UNICORN LEADERSHIP

Find your passion, achieve your goals, and realize your potential

ANNE WITHERSPOON

FOREWORD BY MICHAEL CLINTON

Unicorn Leadership

Published by
Unicorn Leadership, LLC

ISBN: 979-8-9864662-0-0
eISBN: 979-8-9864662-1-7

Copyediting by Kim Bookless
Proofreading by Monti Shalosky
Cover and Interior Design by GKS Creative
Project Management by The Cadence Group

Cover photo by Kelly Williams Photography
Cover hair and makeup by RickyDallas
Hair color by Annie Arriola
Hair cut by Heather Ly

To my parents, John and Sue Ann,
who taught me what it means
to be authentic and resilient

Contents

Foreword

When my friend Anne Witherspoon asked me to read her book, *Unicorn Leadership,* I was curious about her message and what she wanted to bring forth to the world. Anne is the example of a modern-day professional, a C-suite executive with deep real-world experiences and an insatiable appetite for growth and development, as well as a curiosity about the world around her.

Aside from her impressive academic credentials that include an MBA in international trade, she continues to add layers to her life through such coursework as a Certified Change Management Professional and Wharton's Leadership in the 21st Century certificate. Anne is on a constant quest to expand her knowledge and perspective as both a human being and a business leader. But unlike many armchair philosophers, academics, or motivational speakers, she continues to excel every day in her business career, which makes her observations all the more relevant for anyone who wants to move into a deeper professional experience.

I should admit upfront that Anne and I are kindred spirits in that we are both on a quest of lifelong learning in all aspects of our lives. Like her, I've always been a voracious reader of personal improvement and self-help books that might give me insight on becoming a better person or manager or leader. Over a forty-year magazine publishing career, most recently as president and publishing director of Hearst Magazines, it was always with great intent that I wanted to continue to learn how I might become better at leading my teams, as well as learning from them. This was especially true as my industry shifted from a print-centric one to a digital model.

During that transition, I made sure to read a lot about transformation, disruption, and how to keep teams motivated during moments of significant change. Yet many books I read on the subject came off as too pedantic or felt like dense homework assignments. Give me inspiration with real, practical advice that I can put into action! In *Unicorn Leadership,* Anne does just that.

What surprised me the most, as I sat down to read this book, is how it is not only for businesspeople but for all kinds of people who are committed to learning how to become better individuals in general. Filled with wonderful anecdotes of personal experience, Anne takes the reader on a journey of self-reflection, reminding us that the best leaders always have a growth mindset in all aspects of their lives, but as leaders, we are also individuals with real virtues and faults. There is always something new to learn regardless of where we are on life's journey.

Unicorn Leadership will teach you that growth is holistic in that it is not about just performance and efficiency—often the measurements of a leader's success—but also about the importance of compassion and understanding, as well as integrating our true authentic selves into how we lead. That alchemy includes self-compassion, as well as self-care. To be a successful leader, one also has to take care of one's own well-being. In a demanding workplace, that means taking the time for meditation, exercise, sleep, and overall good living habits, only some of the great advice you'll discover in these pages.

But what I really loved about *Unicorn Leadership* is that it is a mix of life coaching and business smarts with a positivity that is contagious. Its references to books that have inspired her, quotes that can become a daily mantra (one of my favorites: If you are always ready, you never have to get ready!), and reminders that we are all people, regardless of our position in a company or industry, are what is unique about this read.

Anne's book will teach you how to become a better human being and leader—no, an extraordinary one. She has done a masterful job of capturing what a twenty-first-century leader should become. Follow the practical and inspirational advice in this book, and you will grow, evolve, excel, and feel fulfillment in both your personal and professional life.

Unicorn Leadership is a reference book you will go back to again and again as you earn your Unicorn stripes, becoming the role model that the author has become for all of us.

MICHAEL CLINTON
New York, New York

Introduction

I've been on a twenty-five-plus-year career journey that has combined book learning with experience. My objective in writing this book is to share both of these with you. I believe leadership is a science and an art. Therefore, I have consumed numerous books, articles, and learnings and tried to put research (science) into action. I have, at times, adjusted various approaches to specific situations (art). But throughout, I have continued to learn, tweak, and improve.

Throughout the book, I reference numerous authors and books that have had a lasting impact on my life and my leadership approach. I am forever grateful to these thought leaders who have provided me with profound guidance and direction in my journey. Their research is invaluable, and their insight is so inspirational. I also share my own experiences and lessons learned along the way. I hope you will find the combination valuable and useful and that you will be able to apply some of this information to your own life and career.

(Book learning + Experiences) + Application to daily life and career = Magic

My hope is that we all take steps to get us closer to a magical journey in life—and one step closer to becoming a Unicorn Leader. I believe becoming a Unicorn Leader is a lifelong pursuit. You never "arrive." There is always work to be done to improve yourself. There is always something more you can do to help others. There is always more to learn. For many years now, I have been on a quest to become the very best leader I could be—who was part of the very best team. Will you join me on this quest?

I'm not sure when the unicorn became an inspiring leadership symbol for me. It was like a perfect storm that was meant to be. It started with me really focusing on the power individual strengths could bring to a team. I tried to get out of the way and let people be the unique beings they are. It became important to focus my efforts on developing myself and ensure everyone around me had access to information and opportunity. (I also took some funny online quizzes about "What is your spirit animal?" Turns out mine is a unicorn.)

Following thought leaders, authors, researchers, speakers, and influencers, I tried to learn all I could to be the best person, and leader, I could be. I read hundreds of books on leadership, teams, emotional intelligence, motivation, management, and inspiration. Implementing research and leveraging actual data helped build team morale and deliver results. Wanting anyone who worked on my team to be the best they could be became my obsession.

Because I was paying closer attention to my career journey—and the journeys of those around me—I became more intentional about my energy and actions. I wanted to ensure I took steps to improve myself and realize my own potential. Realizing your own potential begins with you. It takes some time and work to dig deep into your soul and figure out how you are wired, what brings you joy, what you are passionate about, and what you really want to do in life. I became self-aware enough to know that my own personal limitations could unintentionally have negative impact on others if I didn't spend the time necessary to work on myself. My objective was not perfection but rather continual personal awareness and development. I aspired to be someone who didn't stand in my own way.

I also wanted to take steps to inspire, develop, and facilitate the success of those around me. The leaders, bosses, and managers I have encountered along the way have had an enormous impact on my life—some good and some bad. After years of being in leadership positions, I realized I could have a huge (hopefully positive) impact on people's lives if I took intentional steps to do so. I wanted to help others achieve their goals. Encouraging others to find their passions and do more than they ever thought they could is a priority for me.

Additionally, I realized there is always something you can learn from others. I've had the privilege to work with some amazing people over the years. They have taught me so much and helped me along in my journey. They made me a better person and supported me in challenging times. I've also learned plenty from some not-so-amazing people whose leadership style I would never choose to replicate but who have definitely played a part in getting me to where I am today. (Without question, I wouldn't have as much material if it weren't for them!)

My approach is to use my strengths and the strengths of my team to accomplish significant things and have a lot of fun along the way. As one of my mentors once stated, "I want to do meaningful things with people I like." I've adjusted that a bit for myself: ***I want to go on magical adventures with teams I love.***

I believe this approach just might be a magical thing—like a unicorn.

Continuous self-improvement to reach personal potential

+

Focus on developing and inspiring others to achieve their potential

+

Ongoing learning

=

Unicorn Leadership

Imagine the world of work if all leaders took this formula and implemented research-based approaches to improve their own lives—and the lives of others! It would truly be magical. There would be less stress and burnout and more fulfillment and happiness.

At one point, I was fortunate enough to be part of a dream team. I have experienced the reward and fulfillment of working alongside talented, motivated, and positive people. For that, I am forever grateful. I have learned I can take intentional steps to manifest the universe and create the life I want to live.

Unicorn Leadership is designed to be a handbook with short, bite-sized chapters and forty specific action steps to assist you with your personal journey. May exploring the topics in this book—such as values, teamwork, employee engagement, self-compassion, and authentic leadership—assist you to evolve as a leader. This is a book for anyone who is interested in continuous personal development and believes we can take intentional steps to manifest the universe and create the magical life we all deserve.

Read it start to finish or pick chapters in order of what intrigues you the most. I encourage you to consider implementing some of the approaches included in the Unicorn Leader Action Steps. These are actionable, intentional steps that I believe can assist you in your own personal and professional growth.

I hope you will take time to Map Your (Unicorn Leader) Journey and contemplate the best possible way to attain your goals.

Thank you for joining me on this adventure. Together, we can manifest the universe. Now, let's get started!

CHAPTER ONE

Values

Values are like fingerprints. Nobody's are the same,
but you leave 'em all over everything you do. —ELVIS PRESLEY

Values are foundational. They can serve as your North Star and help direct your journey in leadership and life. Strong leaders are value driven. Their focus, their actions, and their decisions are based on values. Determining your own personal values and the values of your family is foundational. Understanding the values of the organization where you work and the values of the individual team members—and how they align with your own values—will help you achieve greater happiness and success. Let's explore these areas and the steps you can take in your journey to become a strong, value-driven leader.

PERSONAL VALUES

The things that are important to us and the behaviors and characteristics that guide our decisions and motivate us are our personal values. Some people value security and honesty; others may value trust and accountability. Personal values can be hard to determine. It's important to think about what is most important in your life and how you really want to live your life.

My values are: **Family, Happiness, Excellence, Growth, and Leadership.**

For values to be meaningful and actionable, I don't think you should have more than three to five of them. If everything is a "value," then nothing is . . . it makes it too hard to focus and live your values.

It's powerful and life changing when you begin to live your values. You are better able to determine what you will and will not put up with in a job, a relationship, a friendship, and in life. Sometimes, realizing your values comes after particular challenges that make it crystal clear what is most important to you.

Family is one of my core values because of three enlightening reasons:

1. In the past, I have let my selfish behaviors negatively impact my family.
2. On a Tuesday, I found out my mother had only weeks to live; once she passed, my dad moved a few miles down the road from me.
3. One day, I realized my kids had crossed the threshold of having *less* time to live with me than they had already lived with me; they were growing up and would soon be gone.

In the past, if I had been more focused on this value of **Family**, I would have saved myself and others some pain. I would have fewer regrets. But now it is a value, and I prioritize my husband, my dad, and my kids above all else. It makes decisions much easier. Constant travel and work events every night? No thank you. Job opportunity in another city or state? Not right now. Miss a school presentation or event? If at all possible, no. Take my kids on memorable trips? Absolutely! Eat lunch as a family every weekend? Yes! Take vacation during spring break? Yes!

Happiness is one of my core values because I believe life is too short to be miserable. Sure, we all have to do things at times that don't inspire happiness or that we don't really want to do. But the trick is to not let that go on so long that you lose track and can't remember the last time you were really happy. I'm so passionate about happiness, I have taken college courses on it, read countless books, and have an app on my phone.

I selected **Excellence** because at my core, I really want to be the best at whatever I am doing. I believe it is important to give it your all and strive for excellence in all you do—work, family, volunteering, friendships. I truly have a burning desire to be excellent. That's how I want my boss, my employees, my family, my colleagues, and my friends to describe me.

I've realized over the years that **Growth** is one of my values because I do not feel satisfied unless I am learning and moving forward. That's why I have so many certifications. That's why I prefer reading to watching TV. That's why I have read so many books and still have so many left to read. I get bored easily. After a year or so of performing a certain job, I want to know what is next and what can I take on now. Upward and onward!

Leadership is near and dear to me. Have you seen the meme "I'm not bossy, I'm a leader"? Story of my life. Since I was a kid, I've been interested in leading. I've had vision and wanted to pave the way. It was important to me to have a significant impact by helping others, giving, and sacrificing. Wanting to be inspired and to inspire, working *for* those and *with* those who had great leadership skills was significant to me.

Realizing and understanding your personal values is fundamental to moving forward as we look at (1) your family's values, (2) the values of your company, and (3) your team members' values.

FAMILY VALUES

My husband once commented that as much time as I spent reading about business, and how to inspire employees, and how to achieve success in my career, he wondered how much time I had spent studying or learning about how to be a great parent or how to inspire our kids. WOW.

The embarrassing answer was—not very much time at all! So I set about changing that and read multiple books, including *The 5 Love Languages of Children: The Secret to Loving Children Effectively, The 7 Habits of Happy Kids*, and my favorite, *The 3 Big Questions for a Frantic Family: A Leadership Fable . . . About Restoring Sanity to the Most Important Organization in Your Life* by Patrick Lencioni.

Discussing these questions from Patrick Leoncini's book with your family can be a very interesting and enjoyable process. It gives everyone the opportunity to talk about their passions and how you spend your time as a family. The book inspired my family to determine our family's core values: **Love, Laughter, Excellence, Respect, and Teamwork**. Knowing your family values helps you make critical family decisions about how you spend your time and energy. What are your family's core values?

We also created vision boards to help keep focus on our individual goals and dreams. We had a good discussion about many important topics that helped provide clarity, identified some potential areas that were not aligned, and provided an opportunity to course-correct. It's not about having a "perfect" family or doing "perfect" activities. It's about getting on the same page and having an open and ongoing dialogue about the dynamics of your unique family.

After that first initial family conversation, remember to revisit those values and refresh your vision boards periodically. The family dynamic continues to evolve as children grow up, so it is essential to have ongoing discussions to stay aligned.

COMPANY VALUES

Most companies have their values on their walls, websites, mousepads, annual report, awards, and other places. But many companies don't live their values. Sometimes their stated values should be considered table stakes and not necessary to print (for example, if you are an investment company and have to state one of your values is Trustworthy, that might be more concerning than inspiring).

I went on a tour of an Amazon facility and was very impressed by the values written on their walls. "Have a backbone" was interesting and inspiring to me. It seemed very clear and candid.

I've toured Zappos headquarters several times and recommend it to everyone who visits Las Vegas. When you tour the office and learn more about their approach, it is clear they seem to be living their 10 Core Values:

1. Deliver WOW through Service
2. Embrace and Drive Change
3. Create Fun and a Little Weirdness
4. Be Adventurous, Creative, and Open-Minded
5. Pursue Growth and Learning
6. Build Open and Honest Relationships with Communication
7. Build a Positive Team and Family Spirit
8. Do More with Less
9. Be Passionate and Determined
10. Be Humble

I think these are pretty awesome, and they make me want to work at Zappos! They align with my own values of Family, Happiness, Excellence, Growth, and Leadership. If you visit the Zappos headquarters, you will find you can buy T-shirs and other merchandise that highlights Zappos' 10 Core Values. When I visited, I bought the Embrace and Drive Change T-shirt. I love how serious Zappos is about their values and how they incorporate them into all they do. We should all learn from them and ensure we are taking steps to honor and live our own values.

I once worked at a company that revised its values every few years, and each time, we received a new company-sponsored mouse pad. The values went from clear and inspiring to ambiguous and dull over the years. I think I ended up with a mouse pad that had words like Integrity, Respect, and Entrepreneurial. All lovely words, but they did not necessarily motivate me to jump out of bed each morning.

What are the values of the company where you work? List them here:

Do they speak to you? Inspire you? Ask yourself two questions:

1. *Is my company living their values?* If your company has "Employee Care" written on their wall as a core value but has harsh HR policies or workplace standards that don't actually seem to *care* for employees, they are NOT living their values. Anyone can put any word on a wall . . . what matters is how they bring those words to life.

2. *Do my company's values align with my values?* If your company's values include working 24/7 with no recognition of holidays or weekends and your own core value is Family or Balance or Flexibility, this is not in alignment and will not work out well in the long run.

TEAM VALUES

I conducted a team values exercise years ago with one of my teams to help articulate and summarize our departmental values. It was a facilitated effort where we asked for feedback from team members and really thought about what made us unique. We discussed what we thought was important and what motivated us to do great work every day. It was an insightful exercise, and we went through several iterations and feedback sessions to ultimately summarize our values:

- Deliver World Class Service
- Have Fun
- Embrace Change
- United as One Team
- Find a Way to Say Yes

As the leader, I was not involved in these sessions. I did not provide any input in or influence on the outcome. These were values of the people, by the people, and for the people. We asked one of our creative team members to design a laminated card for us, and we passed them out to everyone.

We worked these values into presentations and tried to live them every day. If we had a team member who was not embracing these values, we coached them under the guidance of these values. When we interviewed, we talked about these values and asked candidates to provide examples of how they might act and achieve with these values in mind. We learned our team wasn't for everyone . . . and that was okay. As a result, we had a more cohesive and productive team because we were very clear on our values.

We also conducted exercises to encourage team members to define their own personal values. We documented them, talked about them, and worked them into the fabric of individual meetings and discussions. It was a powerful way to get to know one another better and understand what inspires each person. For a leader, it helps you know how to motivate the individual and the team. You learn to better relate to people and understand their perspective. It helps both of you understand the source of any frustration and conflict.

Do you know your direct reports' core values? If not, I encourage you to go find out and begin taking the time to discuss and learn from one another. If you do know their core values, then you are already on the right path to becoming a Unicorn Leader!

. . . . .

Values are fundamental to becoming a great leader. Spend some time thinking about your personal core values, your family values, your company values, and your team values. Write them down. Discuss them with your work team and your family. Align your values with your organization's values. And most important, live them.

UNICORN LEADER ACTION STEP

Search the example of values below and select your top five. You can also find more options by doing a quick internet search. Write them down and take steps to start living them today. Put some thought into it. Don't select the trendy words, or options that you think would please your mother. Pick the words that speak to your soul.

1. ______________________________

2. ______________________________

3. ______________________________

4. ______________________________

5. ______________________________

Examples of Values

Abundance
Acceptance
Accomplishment
Accuracy
Achievement
Adaptability
Adventure
Affluence
Altruism
Ambition
Amusement
Assertiveness
Attentiveness
Attractiveness
Authenticity
Awareness
Awe
Balance
Beauty
Belonging
Benevolence
Boldness
Bravery
Calmness
Candor
Capability
Celebrity
Certainty
Challenge
Charity
Charm
Chastity
Cheerfulness
Clarity
Cleanliness
Clear-mindedness
Collaboration
Comfort
Commitment
Communication
Community
Compassion
Competence
Connection
Consistency
Contentment
Control
Cooperation
Courage
Creativity
Daring
Decisiveness
Dependability
Determination
Devotion
Diligence
Discipline
Discovery
Diversity
Drive
Duty
Ease
Education
Effectiveness
Efficiency
Elegance
Empathy
Endurance
Ethics
Excellence
Expertise
Fairness
Faith
Fame
Family
Fidelity
Fitness
Focus
Freedom
Friendliness
Friendship
Frugality
Fun
Generosity
Grace
Gratitude
Growth
Happiness
Harmony
Health
Honesty
Honor
Hopefulness
Humility
Humor
Imagination
Impact
Independence
Individuality
Influence
Ingenuity
Inspiration

Intelligence
Intimacy
Inventiveness
Joy
Justice
Kindness
Knowledge
Leadership
Learning
Liberty
Logic
Love
Loyalty
Mastery
Mindfulness
Moderation
Modesty
Neatness
Nerve
Nonconformity
Obedience
Order
Organization
Originality
Passion
Peace
Perfection
Philanthropy
Playfulness
Popularity
Positivity
Power
Precision
Privacy
Professionalism
Prosperity
Quickness
Quietness
Reason
Recognition
Reflection
Relaxation
Religion
Resilience
Respect
Responsibility
Risk
Sacrifice
Satisfaction
Security
Self-Care
Selflessness
Serenity
Service
Sharing
Significance
Simplicity
Sophistication
Spirituality
Stability
Strength
Style
Success
Sympathy
Teamwork
Temperance
Thankfulness
Thoroughness
Thoughtfulness
Tidiness
Timeliness
Tolerance
Traditionalism
Tranquility
Transcendence
Travel
Trustworthiness
Truth
Understanding
Uniqueness
Unity
Usefulness
Value
Variety
Virtue
Vitality
Warmth
Wealth
Wholesomeness
Willingness
Winning
Wisdom
Witty
Wonder
Worthiness
Youthfulness
Zaniness

CHAPTER TWO

Know Yourself

Hide not your talents. They for use were made. What's a sundial in the shade?
—BENJAMIN FRANKLIN

It is critical to understand all the pieces and parts that make up your personality and make you the unique and magical creature you are. To really understand your whole composition, dig a little deeper into your personality and strengths. Get to know what makes you tick, what you love, what you loathe, and why. When you understand your personal characteristics and preferences, you can more easily adjust to various situations and people. When you know yourself and your uniqueness, you can take steps to ensure you are positioned to perform the best work of your life.

UNDERSTAND YOUR PERSONALITY

The first time I remember taking a personality assessment was in my first job after college. As part of a team meeting, we took the "Colors" test where everyone reviewed different selections of words and chose which word was most like them. The results determined whether you were Red, Yellow, Blue, or Green; and the summaries helped illustrate what those personalities represented. (I was the Reddest of the Reds.)

I have taken various similar assessments over the years, including the Social Compass where the results determined your personality style. I've always liked this assessment and found it to be very helpful. *The Social Compass* was written by Gwynne N. Dawdy, PhD, and here's a summary of possible results:

Navigator: motivated by results, achievement, accomplishment, and success

Social Servitor: motivated by connection, team cohesion, belonging, and love

Explorer: motivated by adventure, freedom, and excitement

Worker: motivated by details, goal achievement, results, and stability

I love these types of assessments because they can help with three important things:

- Better understanding of yourself and preferences
- Better understanding of others and their preferences (We are all very different!)
- Better understanding of how to adjust your own approach when interacting with various team members

Taking various assessments as a team and discussing and highlighting results can be very powerful. When you better understand the personality and preferences of your manager, you can adjust your style to better fit hers to improve communication and your relationship. When you better understand the traits of your team members, you can adjust to build rapport and deliver better results. All of this knowledge, when applied, can help avoid miscommunication and misunderstandings.

Once, I had a Unicorn Leader manager who had his direct employees and their direct employees take the Myers-Briggs assessment. Everyone received their detailed results, and then the summary was discussed in a team meeting. A good amount of time was spent discussing what we now understood about each team member and how we could now better perform as an individual and as a team member with this knowledge. It really helped bring the team closer together at that point in time, but it also helped me with a difficult conversation with that leader in the future.

It was a challenging time at work with significant chaos and a splash of dysfunction. I was struggling with how to articulate what I was feeling and exactly why I was struggling—not only how to articulate it to my manager but even to myself. I kept thinking: What is my problem? Why can't I cope with this? Maybe I'm just not ________________ (insert word: talented, capable, smart, good) enough for this job!

I remembered my Myers-Briggs results and dug them out of a file, thinking maybe I could find some insight. Yes! This was exactly what I needed as a reminder to myself and to better communicate with my manager. I am an ESTJ and I:

- have little sympathy for ineffective or inefficient work
- expect fairness and consistency
- do not appreciate actions that waste time
- believe deeds matter and words do not
- abhor confusion

And when my needs are not met, I may become critical, vocal, bossy, and impatient. Under extreme stress, I may withdraw and want to be alone, have intense emotions, and attribute negative meanings to others' actions or statements. Yes!—this is exactly what I was feeling and doing!

Since my manager "spoke Myers-Briggs," I simply read these items off to him at our next meeting, and he got it. He now understood why I had been struggling and why I had become so negative and critical. We both could then take steps to determine how to help me adjust, be able to handle certain situations, and become more successful in the current environment. This is a powerful example of how knowing yourself, knowing others, and utilizing that knowledge can be a game changer.

IDENTIFY YOUR STRENGTHS

Gallup research indicates that people who have the opportunity to focus on their strengths every day are six times as likely to be engaged in their jobs and more than three times as likely to report having an excellent quality of life in general. When you are not utilizing your strengths at work, you are more likely to dread your job, have negative interactions with your colleagues, and achieve less on a daily basis. Clearly, it is very important to focus on our strengths. Unfortunately, most people are unaware of their own strengths. Unicorn Leaders know this to be a source of great power and intentionally focus on their strengths and the strengths of their team.

Taking the StrengthsFinder assessment can be a life-changing experience. From a potential list of thirty-four, the assessment will pinpoint your personal five strengths. This is extremely powerful, because you will not only have a better understanding of yourself but you begin to understand why you enjoy doing certain tasks and jobs and how to best put those strengths into action.

From the StrenghtsFinder assessment, my strengths are:

- Achiever
- Competition
- Focus
- Learner
- Significance

It explains so much. I have an internal fire burning inside of me and a desire to achieve something tangible every single day because I'm an

Achiever. (That's why I'm not good at relaxing. I must produce a tangible result. Every. Day.) As a result of **Competition** as a strength, I don't compete for the fun of it; I compete to win. (Halloween competition? Team sports? Sign me up!) I set goals and am impatient with delays and obstacles, and I am compelled to move toward my destination because of my **Focus.** (It's why I can Get. $hit. Done.) Due to being a **Learner,** I am energized by the steady and deliberate journey from ignorance to competence. (It's why I have multiple professional certifications.) I want to be heard and to be credible, professional, and successful. I am drawn away from the mediocre toward the exceptional by virtue of my strength called **Significance.** (Unicorn Leadership perhaps?)

Another similar assessment I like is from the book *Standout 2.0* by Marcus Buckingham. This assessment narrows down your top two strengths out of nine possible strengths. Combining your results with additional insight from this book will help you identify ways to make an immediate impact, take your performance to the next level, and learn how to manage others with various strengths. My strengths are Creator and Pioneer. As a **Creator**, I love to complete projects, make presentations, and write. I like to organize chaos! As a **Pioneer**, I have a bias for action, and my life is about forward motion and momentum. Yes and Yes!

Being able to understand and articulate your strengths is magical because now you have a clearer vision of why certain jobs or roles that you've had were your favorite and others you simply dreaded. This is powerful, not just for career success but for happiness in life. For most of my life, I thought a strength was something I was good at: basketball, schoolwork and tests, getting a lot of work done in a short amount of time. As I've come to learn from the work of Marcus Buckingham and Ashley Goodall, "something I'm good at" is not a strength; it is an *ability.* A *strength* is "an activity that makes you feel strong." In the book *Nine Lies About Work,* the authors encourage us to think about the activities we do and how those activities make us feel.

We are drawn to activities in which we find joy. The more you are able to focus on activities you love and less on activities you loathe, the stronger, happier, and less prone to burnout you will be.

Think about your past couple of weeks at work. Look at your calendar and assess how you've spent your time. Did you look forward to all of those meetings on your calendar? Did you look forward to working on that project? Which meetings were actually fun? What project work flew by? Which meetings and work activities made you feel great and fulfilled when they were over? After reflecting on this and having a better idea of where your strengths may lie, it's important to try to do more of those things. Reduce or eliminate activities you loathe and increase or do only activities you love—this is an important piece of the Unicorn Leader journey. Utilize your strengths and find joy in your work and in your overall life!

EXPLORE YOUR TEAM STRENGTHS

In the words of Mother Teresa: *"I can do things you cannot, you can do things* I *cannot*; together *we can* do great *things."*

I want to know my team members' strengths so that I can understand them better and help ensure they are in the right role. It helps provide transparency to strengths that overlap and where there is commonality, but also provides insight into where gaps can be filled and who can help another team member when a certain strength is lacking. You can learn details about each strength and put ideas into action. You will be able to get team members into the right roles where they can add the highest value and be the most productive.

It's not enough for me to be aware of each team member's strengths—they should all know each other's strengths. Share your strengths, talk about them in team meetings, provide recognition based on the success their strength was able to help them achieve, and discuss examples of where their particular strength helped solve a certain problem or helped create a specific solution. This is powerful!

Which is more meaningful feedback for a team member?

- "Great job, Dave, on completing this critical initiative!"
- "Great job, Dave! Your Arranger strength allowed you to thrive in a complex situation while aligning variables in the most productive configuration possible. This, combined with your Adaptability strength, allowed you to handle all the sudden requests and remain flexible when the demands of this project pulled you in many different directions at once!"

And chances are, since you knew your team members' strengths, you decided to put Dave in that role. From the beginning, you knew his likelihood of success was very high based on his strengths and what was required of this particular role.

It's a win-win opportunity to understand and incorporate a strength-based approach into any work environment. When you identify and celebrate your team strengths, you are taking the first step toward building a dream team who can achieve great things together.

. . . . .

This may sound like a lot of analysis and work to figure out more about yourself, but I promise you it is worth it. Discovering your personal uniqueness and understanding the details of your strengths can help you better determine your purposeful path in life. I encourage you to take time to assess your personality and strengths and learn your team members' personality and strengths. Knowledge is power, and this knowledge helps you better inspire your team and avoid soul-sucking work and makes it more likely you will enjoy a more magical journey in life.

UNICORN LEADER ACTION STEPS

- You can try a personality assessment today without spending any money and with very little effort. One that I like is the Personality Compass. You can find it at www.leadrighttoday.com. Take it with your team. Is your primary direction North, South, East, or West? Each primary direction has characteristics that naturally fit well with certain jobs, provides insight into your uniqueness, and highlights commonalities you share with others.
- Find the StrengthsFinder 2.0 book on Amazon with a code for the assessment and learn more about how you can begin to use your strengths today. Discover your strengths, make a list, and starting using them.
- I encourage you to take the Standout 2.0 assessment right now at www.marcusbuckingham.com. It doesn't take very long to complete and will give you immediate insight that you can transform into action.
- Take the Zone of Genius quiz. Download tools and the Performance Tracker at www.lauragarnett.com. Spend some time figuring out what your "genius" is and how you can achieve more joy in your work. Use the Performance Tracker in the Genius Habit to help ensure you are using your Genius in all you do and help optimize joy and confidence in your career and life.

CHAPTER THREE

Culture

The culture of any organization is shaped by the worst behavior the leader is willing to tolerate. —TODD WHITAKER

Company culture is the mission, shared values, attributes, and characteristics of an organization. It can be tangible or intangible. Sometimes it is transparent and obvious; other times it is more nuanced and hiding in the shadows. You know it when it's great; and when it's bad, it can wreak havoc. Almost every company claims to want to have a great corporate culture, but very few actually achieve it.

Culture starts with the founders and evolves from there. It can proceed from good to great, but it can also fall apart along the way or morph into something else entirely. It's fascinating to watch, learn, and witness various outcomes a corporate culture can determine. By more closely examining mission statements and reviewing tangible and intangible items, we can get a better idea of the true culture. We must also pay attention to the feelings or "vibes" we get and the intentionality we experience at an organization to have clarity about the culture.

MISSION STATEMENT

You can tell a lot by a company's mission statement. Some are really spot on and inspirational and leave no doubt what that company is all about.

Here are some of my favorites. Do you recognize them?

1. To live and deliver WOW (Zappos)
2. We aim to be Earth's most customer-centric company (Amazon)
3. Never Stop Growing (MPA)

What about these?

- To challenge the status quo. To think different (Apple)
- To create happiness for people of all ages, everywhere (Disney)
- To empower every person and organization on the planet to achieve more (Microsoft)
- To refresh the world and inspire moments of optimism and happiness (Coca-Cola)

What is your company's mission statement?

Is it clear? Inspirational? Does it speak to your soul and motivate you to achieve the mission? If so, that is something to celebrate, but let's dig a bit deeper into this topic.

Let's say you have a clear, inspiring, and motivating mission statement. But is the company living that mission? Do the investments align with the statement? Do the projects and initiatives support that mission or stray from that mission?

TANGIBLE ITEMS

What are some tangible items that illustrate and embody a company's culture?

- Free soda, free food, free coffee (maybe even "good" coffee) in the break room
- Casual Friday or Casual Everyday
- Christmas or annual bonus
- Number of vacation days and overall vacation policy
- Work from home policy
- Stock awards policy
- On-site gym or workout facility
- Reserved parking spaces for officer level employees
- Size and location of offices for various managers
- Milestone work anniversary recognition
- Transparency in communication and visibility into organizational structure
- Others?

List the tangible items of your company's culture:

____

____

____

These are easy to see and easy to determine their existence. They allow a potential or existing employee the opportunity to decide whether these are meaningful aspects of any job. What is more challenging to determine are the intangible items of a company culture.

INTANGIBLE ITEMS

These are things that you can't quite put your finger on or are more challenging to articulate but that you feel or experience in your daily existence. As Herb Kelleher said, "Culture is what people do when no one is looking."

- Do you get a different vibe when you go to different floors in your building? Does one floor seem particularly positive or upbeat and another floor seems depressing? That is the individual department culture you are feeling.
- How about when important decisions are made and communicated? Do those decisions sometimes get reversed because some people have a back channel to the top and are able to influence certain outcomes?
- Are certain behaviors tolerated or allowed to occur within some groups but not others? How does your frontline sales organization treat your back office or support teams?
- How do you feel after you leave certain meetings—inspired, fulfilled, and engaged? Or demotivated, discouraged, and uncertain?

It's important to pay attention to all the vibes throughout your day, week, and year and continuously assess whether you feel positive and inspired by your daily work or you feel cynical and unengaged. These feelings can add up and either propel you forward and allow you to perform at your very best or drag you down, create self-doubt, and lower performance.

I used to work at a company where the culture had become so dysfunctional, I could actually feel the negativity and bad vibes to my core as I walked down the hallway at the corporate headquarters. I felt like I was covered with a blanket of dread and despair. Pay attention to those feelings and, if possible, take action to get out of those environments!

Think about the intangible items of your company's culture. Are you able to articulate them and list them here?

GOOD VIBES ONLY

You can rarely control the corporate culture in which you find yourself immersed, but you can generally control many aspects of the culture of the teams you lead. This is where you have the opportunity to make a difference in the lives of people—a positive and meaningful difference. You, as a leader, can set the tone for what will and will not be tolerated.

One thing I have strongly discouraged is a DIVA Mentality. You can't inspire teams to achieve, or to collaborate, if a DIVA Mentality is tolerated. I came up with this acronym years ago when I was working on a project where the DIVA mentality was so prevalent and was placing a huge obstacle in the way of team success.

What is a DIVA Mentality?

D: Destroy the morale of those around you with your actions

I : Me, myself, and I (you think it's all about you)

V: VIP approach (everything is a rush because you are very important)

A: ADD (you can't focus, can't follow a process, can't complete a task you said was very important last week)

Additionally, I am very opposed to energy vampires and at one time posted signs all around our floor that said: "No Energy Vampires Allowed." Energy vampires are people who drain your energy and surround themselves with negativity. You must avoid these people and do your best to not allow them on your team. They will suck the life and positivity right out of you.

Over the years of being a people manager, I've seen that most performance issues were rarely caused by lack of skill or ability but instead were caused by behavior or attitude. It was always more challenging to have coaching discussions with people because behavior can be so subjective and personal. What I find to be unacceptable behavior, you might think is okay. It's much easier to deal with skill or ability issues because they are objective. If Dave is supposed to be at work by 8:30 but always arrives at 8:45, I can say, "Dave, you need to be here by 8:30, not 8:45, and I need you to make sure you are here by 8:30." If Dave is supposed to produce fifteen widgets a day and is only producing ten widgets a day, I can say, "Dave, you need to produce fifteen widgets, not ten widgets. Is there some reason you are not able to produce fifteen widgets? What can I do to help? How can we work together to produce fifteen widgets?"

But if Dave just rubs people the wrong way and is generally not a person others want to work with, it's harder to coach Dave on that. What do you say? "Dave, please change so people actually like you?" Probably not. However, I am happy to say there is a solution. In the book *The Ideal Team Player* by Patrick Lencioni, it is brilliantly explained that Dave may be a jackass! That sounds really harsh, doesn't it? But what it really means is Dave isn't very humble, very hungry, and/or very people smart . . . and THAT is why people generally don't like him and find his behavior unacceptable. His behavior is bringing down the productivity of the team and is harming the positivity and good vibes of the team.

And now, if you have every team member read the book and discuss the concepts, we all have common language for behavior. When we all learn the virtues of an Ideal Team Player, we can all understand certain behaviors, have discussions about them, and aspire to be better. We can more quickly identify jackasses and take steps not to hire them, fire them more quickly, and create a stronger, healthier team. This makes expectations so much clearer and conversations so much easier.

I once had a Unicorn Leader who not only had his entire team (500-plus) read this book but also required every employee to complete the self-assessment and discuss it with their manager to help ensure every single person was on the same page. He also ensured every new employee received and read the book as well. And he incorporated the concepts into recognition events, discussed the virtues regularly in team meetings, and made these virtues nonnegotiable.

I put together a presentation on this concept highlighting Alexander Hamilton. (Note: here's where I combined two of my loves—the musical *Hamilton* + leadership concepts = bliss.) Hamilton was brilliant, came from nothing, never stopped working, was ambitious, and accomplished a lot. But he wasn't very humble, struggled with being "people smart," and was essentially the Bulldozer. He clearly made some enemies and some very bad decisions, which led to him being killed in a duel. And, to continue "geeking out" on this concept, I would say Aaron Burr was the Skillful Politician. Feel free to reach out to me on this topic; I would love to dig in deeper on this analogy!

I had a great leader on my team who created an Ideal Team Player vision board and would encourage his team to add to it. They would focus on different concepts and topics periodically and together would build out the visuals on the board. It was very effective. The entire floor benefited from this exercise—not just his immediate team—because everyone could see it, would talk about it, and ask about it, and this helped multiply the focus of the concept of being an Ideal Team Player.

I encourage you to use creative ways to underscore concepts for your team. It definitely makes it more tangible and effective when you are able to do this.

What are actions you can take to create good vibes on your team? How can you all be on the same page about behavior and what will or will not be tolerated? I encourage you to take steps to recruit and retain Ideal Team Players and then be very intentional about your culture.

BE INTENTIONAL

If you aren't careful, a great culture can go from good to bad very quickly. The soul and inspiration of the founders that made it a great place to work somehow fades away and gets lost in translation. One of the main reasons for that is because the organization is listening to the wrong voices. "What you hear depends on whom you listen to," says Chris Zook and James Allen in *The Founder's Mentality: How to Overcome the Predictable Crises of Growth.* The great cultures that some founders are able to create can be derailed by growth and other headwinds, so it's critical that you pay close attention to your culture and the very soul of your organization.

And please remember that engaged employees will go the extra mile for the company, the customer, and fellow employees. One study found that engaged employees are 4.7 times more likely than the average to recommend the company to a friend, 3.5 times more likely to make suggestions about how to improve the business, and 3.5 times more likely to take initiative to do something positive that was not expected of them. Please pay attention to your culture and how you are treating employees! Do you lift them up—or tear them down?

As Simon Sinek points out in the book *Leaders Eat Last,* in a weak culture, we veer away from doing "the right thing" in favor of doing "the thing that's right for me." If your organization has a CEO that is "I before You and Me before We," it's a red flag that your culture is moving in the wrong direction.

You can always listen and learn from senior leaders to understand the actual culture. At one company I worked for, the rationale behind some proposed organizational changes were summed up as "one throat to choke." I once had the "privilege" of attending a meeting where it was stated multiple times that "many careers were *ended* with a similar initiative." Well, I guess that makes it particularly clear—clear that:

- Someone is always to blame.
- Someone will be thrown under the bus when things go awry.
- No one should feel safe.
- Failure (and learning) is not allowed.

Watch your language, leaders! Unicorns won't stand for such language and treatment. And you will be left with a lot of silent horses who can't innovate, create, and grow. Treat your team with the respect and inspiration they deserve.

. • . . .

Now that you have a greater awareness of the components of culture, you are better equipped to determine whether your company's culture is a "fit" for you. Do your core values align? Are your strengths being utilized? Does your company's mission statement speak to your soul? Do the tangible and intangible items of your company lift you up or tear you down?

And what type of culture are you creating with your team? You have the power to inspire or intimidate. You have the ability to allow someone to thrive or barely survive. Do people willingly follow you because you are lifting them up—or do they begrudgingly follow you because you have beaten them down?

Contemplating the answers to these questions can help you move forward on your Unicorn Leadership journey with more confidence and clarity.

UNICORN LEADER ACTION STEPS

- Read *The Ideal Team Player: How to Recognize and Cultivate the Three Essetial Virtues* by Patrick M. Leoncini. Encourage (or require) every team member to read it as well. You can find resources and more information at www.tablegroup.com.
- Take the Founder's Mentality diagnostic survey at media.bain.com/founders-mentality/. This can help provide some insight on the current state of your company and culture.

CHAPTER FOUR

Teamwork

Teamwork is not a preference; it's a requirement.
—JOHN WOODEN

The very best leaders do things differently. They understand the importance of teamwork and how teams that work together effectively are able to accomplish incredible things. What if I told you I could practically guarantee you would never lose a high performer by just being more intentional and consistent and thoughtful in your approach as a leader? When you focus on the activities that create a strong workplace and take action to avoid dysfunction, you don't have to worry about people leaving. When you ensure you are developing and recognizing your team, you have the ability to build something very unique. When you treat employees as your most valuable assets (that they are) and give them the attention they need, magical things occur.

TWELVE QUESTIONS

Back in the early 2000s, I had not been out of college for even ten years and had held jobs only as an individual contributor. I was happily selected to attend a "Managerial-Supervisory College" at my place of employment. As part of that focus, we were provided with suggested books to read. One that I happened to select was *First, Break all the Rules* by Marcus Buckingham. It was truly life changing and has been foundational for me in my quest to be the best leader I could be and build the best teams. It also initiated my love of Marcus Buckingham! It was in this book that I discovered that research has proven "the strength of a workplace can be simplified to twelve questions." Twelve questions? It's like finding the secrets of the universe! The questions involve everything from expectations, to opinions, to quality, to having a best friend at work.

Research has shown that every question was linked to productivity, profitability, retention, and customer satisfaction. So, if you are interested in building a strong and productive team, you need to focus on ensuring everyone can answer "Strongly Agree" to as many of these twelve questions as possible.

I read Marcus's book twenty years ago and, since then, have incorporated these questions into my day-to-day leadership. I have asked teams I have led at different organizations and in different roles these questions to better focus on what needs to be tweaked to ensure we have the strongest, most engaged, and most productive team ever! And from time to time, I ask them of myself and gauge what I might be missing in a certain situation so I can try to take steps to improve my own performance and engagement.

Have you heard of these questions? Have you utilized them to help the teams you are leading? I've never come across another leader who has, so please contact me if you have—I would love to connect and learn from you.

This was also the first time I remember learning about the importance of individual strengths and of letting each person determine their own route toward the desired outcome. And there are many other amazing approaches that I still use today. This book planted so many seeds that helped me get on a productive path from day one as a leader and manager. I urge every single leader to read Marcus's book today to help ensure increased success and improved team engagement.

Fast forward twenty years, and these same questions were part of the findings and additional research of Jim Clifton and Jim Harter in the book *It's the Manager*. The questions have also been revisited by Marcus Buckingham and Ashley Goodall in the book *Nine Lies About Work*.

If the twelve questions are still relevant twenty years later, I think we should all pay closer attention.

Research and proven methodology can guide the way for us as leaders and help organizations achieve the desired results, yet so many continue on without this focus and continue to wonder why they aren't successful. Imagine how magical the world could be if we had better leaders, more engaged employees, and more successful organizations! A unicorn can dream . . .

CREATE A SAFE ENVIRONMENT AND AVOID DYSFUNCTION

As Paul Santagata at Google says, "There's no team without trust." Google spent millions on the Project Aristotle initiative to determine what makes a successful team. The number one factor: psychological safety.

Psychological safety is a team climate that is characterized by personal trust and mutual respect, and one in which people are comfortable being themselves. Team members feel like they can speak up without fear of rejection, humiliation, or punishment. Ideas are encouraged and welcomed from all team members. Team members have confidence that they can be authentic and are able to contribute their best work. As Simon Sinek says, "A team is not a group of people who work together. A team is a group of people who trust each other."

As Patrick Lencioni explains in the book *The Five Dysfunctions of a Team*, "Absence of trust stems from the unwillingness to be vulnerable. Team members who are not genuinely open with one another about their mistakes and weaknesses make it impossible to build a foundation for trust."

As a leader, you must ensure you are consistently taking steps to build trust. Every. Day. It takes time and intentional action. And then, the real test comes when there is a "crisis" and your team sees how you respond. Do you throw them under the bus? Work through it together? These scenarios determine whether your team grows stronger or is torn apart.

For over a decade now, I have used methodology to try very hard to avoid—or at least minimize—team dysfunction. You simply cannot achieve what you need to as a team if you are distracted by ongoing dysfunction that results from lack of trust, conflict avoidance, or not holding one another accountable.

One of the first and easiest things to do is just get to know your team! Learn where they are from, what hobbies they enjoy, how many siblings they had, where they went to school, what their favorite sports teams are, their favorite vacation spot, whether or not they have kids (or fur babies), their favorite book, etc.

Schedule unstructured but intentional time to eat, drink, and talk. Maybe throw in some fun to bring certain personalities out into the open. One of my favorite team events was National Have Fun at Work Day (January 28). We always had snacks and a splash of fun, and one year we brought in an arcade dual basketball hoop game. I learned that one of our team members was crazy competitive—more competitive than I am—and before then, I had no idea! It was so fun and enlightening to watch her intensity and joy as she shot basket after basket and won game after game.

Spend time with your team. Get to know them. Build trust.

Another activity I highly recommend is taking *The Five Dysfunctions of a Team* assessment. Through this exercise, you can determine your team's level of trust, commitment, accountability, and more. Teams that I have led take this assessment periodically over the years and discuss results of how we feel about many things. We learn how comfortable we are (or not) with addressing one another's unproductive behaviors and how open we are (or not) to admitting our own weaknesses and mistakes.

It can be very enlightening, but it can also uncover a lot of sensitive topics, so you must be prepared to address them in a caring but direct manner. This is really hard. It's not easy to open yourself up and be vulnerable, but with intentional effort and an ongoing effort to build trust, the strong bond you can build as a team can be a game changer.

CELEBRATE AND RECOGNIZE YOUR TEAM

Do you know your team members' birthdays? Work anniversaries? These are two dates I think every leader should know. These two dates should be recognized and celebrated in some way. For years, I would hand write thank-you notes to each and every team member on their work anniversary date. A handwritten note is almost as rare as a unicorn these days. Try to do something extra special for milestone work anniversaries. When people spend five, ten, and more years at your organization, they should be given extra-special recognition for devoting so much time out of their life.

Having a monthly team celebration that highlights the birthdays and anniversaries of that month is a great way to recognize individuals and bring the team together for some bonding and fun. Consider having different themes, allowing different departments to host, and adding in some other fun activities. For example, in December, you could have cookie decorating contests as part of the monthly celebration. Be creative! Allow others the opportunity to be creative.

Do you know things your team members like? Do they prefer Sonic to Starbucks? Target to Walmart? What is their favorite restaurant? Favorite beverage? Favorite candy? Favorite flower? Do they like cake or pie? Cane's or Chick-fil-A? When you ask these questions, you accomplish two things:

- You have learned more about your team.
- You have shown you care about them as unique individuals.
- You have the opportunity to give them something on special occasions that they actually like and would want.

EMPLOYEES ARE YOUR MOST VALUABLE ASSET

Once, I had a manager who would say, "Employees are our most valuable asset," and then would ask people, "Why are you so stupid?" in meetings. That is definitely not the way to demonstrate your belief in employees as valuable assets.

I believe that having the RIGHT people on your team, and treating them like they are valued, is nonnegotiable. You cannot build a great team or a great organization unless you take this approach.

Consider this question: *Who on your team today, if they resigned, would cause you to have a panic attack, get sick to your stomach, or ______________________ (insert reaction)?* I'm sure a name or two or three popped immediately into your head. Now, for the follow-up question: *What are you doing to ensure they know how valuable you think they are?* Leaders must consistently take intentional steps to treat employees like the most valuable assets they are. Here are some suggested ways to do that:

- Meet one-on-one with them every week
- Tell them "Thank you," or "I couldn't do it without you," or "You are so critical to the success of the team"
- Ask them, "How are you doing?" or "Is there anything I can do to help?"
- Know their answers to the twelve questions
- Conduct "Stay Interviews"

PEOPLE NEED ATTENTION

Research has shown that employees respond to attention. Productivity increases when leaders simply give employees attention. Any attention will do, but ***positive*** attention is more powerful than negative attention in creating high performance on a team. So if you never meet with your team, or talk to your team, or get to know your team until something goes wrong, you are simply not getting the most out of your team. Don't just meet with them or coach them or counsel them when they are struggling or doing things "wrong"; meet with them consistently, tell them what they are doing right, thank them for all that they are doing, and continue to build trust with them.

Positive attention helps us become more engaged and productive. Focusing on strengths and what someone is doing well helps foster growth. Everyone deserves the opportunity to be more engaged and more productive and to grow. Leaders should realize the part they play in allowing that to happen and take steps to provide the attention needed for employees to thrive.

STAY INTERVIEWS

Have you ever conducted a Stay Interview? If not, why not? It's a great way to give attention to your employees, learn about them, build trust, reduce attrition, and find new ways of working. It's important to proactively focus on retaining your most valuable asset. Don't wait until it's too late.

Here's an example of Stay Interview questions I have used in the past:

- What about your job makes you want to jump out of bed in the morning?
- What about your job makes you want to hit the snooze button?
- What can I do to better support you? How can I better recognize your work?

- What can I do more of or less of as your manager?
- What might tempt you to leave this organization?

I was very inspired by *The Book of Beautiful Questions: The Powerful Questions That Will Help You Decide, Create, Connect, and Lead* by Warren Berger. He provides so many various and thoughtful questions that can really help you get to know people at a deeper level. I once gave my direct report employees a list of twenty questions from this amazing book and then took them to lunch to individually review their answers. It was so insightful and helped bring further awareness and understanding to our relationship. I was provided with feedback on their perspective of likes and dislikes, happiness and regret, proud moments and lessons learned. I am certain this exercise and resulting knowledge is one reason we all had such a strong bond.

You can incorporate these questions into weekly touchpoint meetings or lunches or have a dedicated meeting just for these questions. I generally like to provide them ahead of time so people can contemplate their responses.

I also really enjoy having a discussion with my team at the end of the year to assess the previous year and plan for the next year. Here's an example of a Year End Touchpoint discussion:

- How do you think this year went?
- What is your overall satisfaction with your job?
- What part of your job do you enjoy? What part do you not enjoy?
- How can I help you achieve your goals?
- Who are your mentors/champions/sponsors?

Have you ever had a manager ask you questions like these? I haven't. Not in almost thirty years of work. Ever. We can do better! Employees deserve more from their leaders! Get to know your team members today.

Build trust. Pay attention. Increase productivity. Help each other do magical things together!

DEVELOP YOUR TEAM

One of the most important things you can do for your team is to help develop them. Incorporate learning into your team meetings. Provide opportunities—and the budget—for team members to attend conferences, training sessions, and webinars. Encourage curiosity and a growth mindset.

I love to read. I read to learn, to relax, to grow, to laugh, to think, and to be better. However, many people don't enjoy reading, including some of my many team members. When I find really important information, I don't just recommend a book. I take the time to create a summary or presentation to highlight the most important aspects and provide the entire team with an easy-to-digest and easy-to-implement format.

When your team members attend conferences or training, require that highlights and best practices be brought back to the team. Create a multiplier effect by sharing information. We had a saying at one organization that "sharing is caring"! Incorporate that mentality into your everyday work life to help your team become stronger and more knowledgeable.

The most successful companies invest heavily in training and team development. I've been particularly inspired by the Walt Disney Company's focus on this as part of the Disney University. In the program Disney created, "Employee education and development are indispensable components of organizational culture, that is simple enough to remember and act upon, and implemented at all organizational levels." This focus played a huge role in the history and culture of the Walt Disney Company, and I'm sure it could create tangible business results within all companies.

The best teams are created over time and grow strong with the proper amount of understanding, attention, sharing, and caring. When you take intentional steps to learn more about the people you spend much of your life with and take action to bring them closer together, you are more likely to truly enjoy your time at work and be proud of what you accomplish together. When you have awareness of what motivates them and what matters to them, you are able to position them for greater success and know how to celebrate them in a meaningful way. Teamwork is the secret to making the dream work.

UNICORN LEADER ACTION STEPS

- Ask your team the twelve questions from the book *First, Break All the Rules.* Assess the current engagement level of your team and identify areas that require further attention. Work together to address gaps or areas of disengagement. Do all of this in a safe, confidential, and supportive way.
- Together with your team, complete *The Five Dysfunctions of a Team* assessment. You can find this assessment and more information at www.tablegroup.com.
- Arrange a nonwork outing for the team. The options are endless and can be anything: community service, lunch, bowling, painting, or a walk in the park. Provide an opportunity to create bonding experiences.
- Ask each team member to compile a list of their favorite things and use it to provide small gifts and treats on their special days.
- Ask your team members questions to get to know them and better understand what motivates them and keeps them engaged. Use the examples provided above or find other examples by a quick Google of "Stay Interview." At the very least, ask their birthday and know their work anniversary and be sure to recognize them.

CHAPTER FIVE

Have Fun

Most of my life, I have done what I wanted to do. I have had fun on the job.
—WALT DISNEY

Unicorn Leaders know life's too short to not have fun at work. We spend the majority of our lives at work, so it's important to have some fun while we are there. It is a soul-sucking existence to just clock in and clock out and never smile, laugh, or be silly in between. I say a big "No, thank you!" to that.

Yes, work is a serious endeavor. But it doesn't have to be an endeavor without joy, without fun, and without a splash of weirdness. Let your team have some fun. Let yourself have some fun. You might be surprised at the amount of creativity that is unleashed and the improved results you achieve just by allowing a bit of fun into the office. What are some activities you can do to make work more fun? A strong leader knows how to create fun and play.

FUN ACTIVITIES

There are infinite ways to have fun in the office. Below are a few examples. How many of these have you participated in, encouraged your team to do, or just allowed to unfold? Give yourself one point for each item you have experienced at work:

- Had a "pie in the face" event where employees voted which managers got to have pie in their face and then the team gathered around to watch the actual event
- Participated in a team Halloween costume contest
- Won a team Halloween costume contest
- Won a team Halloween costume contest five years in a row (give yourself five extra points for this one!)
- Bet one another a hundred dollars on whether someone could eat ten huge tacos in one hour
- Hosted a race on top of the corporate parking garage to see which team member could back up their bragging of being "the fastest"
- Hosted team happy hours
- Provided breakfast, lunch, and/or snacks on a regular basis
- Celebrated National Fun at Work Day (the last Friday in January)
- Celebrated National High Five Day (the third Thursday in April)
- Brought freeze-dried tarantulas, crickets, and other weird creatures for your team members to eat
- Incorporated periodic awards, recognition, silly trophies, and prizes into critical projects
- Distributed fun award ribbons with unicorns that stated, "You're one of a kind" (AdultingFTW.com)
- Hosted team painting, crafting, bowling, or other sporting events

- Celebrated National Customer Service Week (the first week of October)
- Gave prizes and gift cards to those who could answer the most correct questions about their team members
- Facilitated regular random gift card drawings
- Created a "Wall of Positivity" and encouraged everyone to add their pictures, inspiration, and other items to it
- Created a "Wall of Gratitude" to highlight items the team was thankful for and people they were grateful for in their lives
- Mailed team members thoughtful cards, fun bookmarks, or creative gifts
- Had a team competition to create the best gingerbread house
- Gifted team members with unicorn stickers, fun sticky notes, and/or notebooks labeled "Evil plans and unicorn drawings"
- Created videos of team members cheering or acting out ideal behavior or other zany activities and regularly showed them in team meetings
- Coordinated monthly team birthday/work anniversary parties
- Other: Insert your own examples here. Also, send examples to me—I love inspiration from others!

1-5 points:	You need to add more fun at work ASAP!
6-10 points:	Not too bad, but you can do better!
11-20 points:	Excellent work! Good vibes and team spirit are flowing at your workplace.
25+ points:	You just might be a Unicorn Leader!

Research has shown numerous benefits for employees in fun work environments:

- Increases willingness to try new things and not stress about mistakes they may make
- Increases employee resilience and optimism
- Creates an environment for learning among colleagues
- Encourages group cohesion, better connection, and increased collaboration

CREATE FUN AND PLAY

One of my heroes is the late Tony Hsieh, the founder and former CEO of Zappos. One of the Zappos 10 Core Values is "Create Fun and a Little Weirdness." As he stated in his book, *Delivering Happiness,* "We don't want to become one of those big companies that feel corporate and boring. We want to be able to laugh at ourselves. We look for both fun and humor in our daily work. We want just a touch of weirdness to make life more interesting and fun for everyone. We want the company to have a unique and memorable personality. When you combine a little weirdness with making sure everyone is also having fun at work, it ends up being a win-win for everyone. Employees are more engaged in the work that they do, and the company as a whole becomes more innovative."

One hundred percent Yes!

Have you heard about the **FISH!** Philosophy? One of the **FISH!** principles is to PLAY! Teams that incorporate having fun with their job can positively affect the atmosphere in any busy office and make even the most mundane tasks enjoyable.

The **FISH!** Philosophy originated from documentary filmmaker John Christensen. He was shopping in Seattle when he heard cheering in the distance. Curious, he followed the sound and encountered a crowd surrounding a small fish market—Pike Place Fish Market. Suddenly a fishmonger threw a slippery fish to a coworker, who made a spectacular one-handed catch as the crowd applauded. He invited a delighted customer to catch a fish. Everyone was smiling and buying a lot of fish. John noticed that selling fish looked cold and exhausting, yet these guys were having fun. They attacked their work with energy and engagement. He wondered, *How do they do it?*

Pike Place Fish Market has incorporated fun into their work, and it has paid off by improving employee engagement and retention and customer service. The FISH! Philosophy has principles to help inspire people to be present, incorporate fun and play into their work, and enjoy their day and bring joy to their customers. When you are intentional about your attitude and how you approach things, it can be a game changer.

Organizations around the world have utilized the FISH! Philosophy to increase morale, improve teamwork, and boost effectiveness. I have used these tools and resources with teams I have led before. We not only provided the FISH! Philosophy training, we provided goldfish and gummy fish snacks throughout the day. We gave everyone a fish magnet to remind them to apply this philosophy each day at work. It was a really fun and motivating training, and I would encourage any team to consider it.

Tap into your natural way of being creative and enthusiastic and having fun. Play is the spirit that drives the curious mind, as in "Let's play with that idea!" You can really bring this mindset to everything you do. Have fun at work! Your team deserves to have fun.

• • • • •

Unicorn Leaders know the more fun we can add throughout our working days, the less we will dread work. Having fun at work gives us something to look forward to, fosters friendships, encourages laughter, reduces stress, and drives team engagement. It won't detract from the work that needs to get done or the results you are held accountable for achieving. Instead, it will make that work a bit more enjoyable and the results that much sweeter.

UNICORN LEADER ACTION STEPS

- Plan for some fun at work. Something! Anything! Just incorporate some fun. Search for National Fun Holidays as a starting point and consider providing some tasty snacks for your team on National Apple Pie Day (May 13). Perhaps consider celebrating National Unicorn Day (April 9).
- Put some Play into your workday! Learn more about the FISH! philosophy at www.fishphilosophy.com.

CHAPTER SIX

Provide Feedback

Being a good boss is hard for everyone, no matter how successful they appear on the outside. —KIM SCOTT

Providing productive and constructive feedback is difficult. When we are compassionate human beings, we care about others and may find it challenging to tell them the truth. But they need to know, so they can be better and do better. If you really care about them—as an employee, a friend, or just as a human being—you owe it to them to let them know in a kind but direct way. It can be done, but it is definitely hard. And in the end, it is definitely worth it. When you provide caring and candid feedback, you are helping individuals and the team live up to their potential and achieve greater success.

RADICAL CANDOR

According to the book *Radical Candor: How to Get What You Want* by Kim Scott:

Caring Personally + Challenging Directly = Radical Candor

The very best leaders do this. It's hard. It can be uncomfortable. But it all goes back to trust—and truly caring for your team members. When feedback comes from a place of caring, it's much more effective and productive.

Think about this: Do you tell someone at lunch that they have spinach in their teeth?

If so, why? You are probably close to that person and don't want them to go the rest of the lunch or into the afternoon with a huge green thing stuck in their teeth. You care about them and know that would be embarrassing for them. You know they have an important meeting after this lunch and would be horrified to meet their new client with spinach stuck in their teeth. You want them to succeed. You want to protect them and help them in any way to be successful. This is Radical Candor. Caring and direct feedback.

If you choose not to tell the person they have spinach in their teeth, why is that? You aren't that close? You think it will embarrass them (Ruinous Empathy)? You will be embarrassed (Manipulative Insincerity)? Maybe you think it's funny and can't wait for them to realize it later after meeting with new clients (Obnoxious Aggression)? These are very undesirable options for all involved. Choose Radical Candor! Caring and direct feedback is always the best choice—maybe not the easiest but definitely the best.

As Kim Scott writes in *Radical Candor*, most of us start at Ruinous Empathy. We are generally nice people! Growing up, we have been taught to "not say anything if you can't say something nice," and most of us do not want to hurt someone's feelings. But when you truly care about someone, they deserve to hear feedback.

I'll share a personal example that I am saddened to admit. One day, I was waiting on the elevator, and a male team member came up beside me. We said hello and chatted a bit, and I then noticed his fly was down. So many thoughts went through my head in quick succession: *Oh no! I should tell him . . . I can't tell this male employee of mine his fly is down; he will think I was looking at him 'down there' . . . He will be horrified that his manager's manager saw this . . . Oh no! I don't want him to walk around with his fly down . . . Ugh! . . .* And then the elevator came, and I got on and never told him.

So I landed somewhere between Ruinous Empathy and Manipulative Insincerity because I was too worried about both of us being embarrassed to just whisper, "Your fly is down." I am truly disappointed in myself and hope to be better and do better in future similar situations.

Here's another personal example, somewhat similar to one Kim Scott shares in *Radical Candor* about her interaction with Sheryl Sandberg years ago, when Sheryl told Kim she said "um" too often in a presentation and it made her sound less professional and less intelligent than she actually was:

A colleague and I were doing multiple presentations at different corporate locations. Same presentation, different place, different day—you may know the drill. During his portion of the presentation at the first location, I noticed he kept saying "and things of that nature." I thought, *Well, he's a bit nervous. It's our first presentation of this series—probably a one-off situation,* and I didn't say anything. At the next presentation, he did the same thing. I think I counted at least five or six times that "and things of that nature" was said. So, after that presentation, I told him.

We had worked together for years; we were close and had a good relationship built on trust. I knew it might embarrass him briefly but realized he would want to know and would ultimately appreciate my Radical Candor. He actually didn't believe it at first! He told me there was no way he had said that so many times. I told him that he did and should record himself at the next presentation just to hear for himself.

At the next presentation, he recorded his portion, and afterward, we listened to it together. There it was: "and things of that nature" stated at least five times. He was shocked but couldn't dispute it. Now that he was aware, he could take steps to improve and catch himself the next time. And he did! He improved the quality of his work because I cared enough to provide honest and productive feedback. This is powerful stuff.

BE SUPPORTIVE AND CLEAR

The book *American Icon: Alan Mulally and the Fight to Save Ford Motor Company* tells the story of how Alan Mulally led Ford Motor Company from the brink of bankruptcy to stunning success. Alan Mulally restructured the company and overcame extreme corporate dysfunction. He did it with a lot of radical candor. To help accomplish this task, he posted a list of ten rules on the boardroom wall as a reminder for everyone to put people first, be clear, use facts and data, respect and listen to each other, and have fun—among other things.

I was fortunate enough to hear Alan Mulally speak twice at a conference (The UnConference 2019 and 2020). He told the story about how he would communicate with his team members who resisted the direction he was going with the company, who were stuck in their traditional passive-aggressive behavior, and who thought the required executive business review meetings were a waste of time. He would say, "That's okay. You don't have to come to the meetings. I mean, you can't be part of the Ford team if you don't, but it's okay. It doesn't mean you are a bad person." He would tell them, "You don't have to do these things I'm asking. You will need to not work here anymore, but I'll still love you."

If you have ever seen Alan Mulally speak, you know he is the most humble, calm, and genuine person. He definitely walks the talk when he puts "People first" on a list. He cares personally about his team members, but he doesn't shy away from confrontation, and he challenges directly. The best leaders do this, and he is definitely one of the very best.

PROVIDE THE EXAMPLE

I once found myself in a very overwhelming situation at work. I was already working at full capacity, but my boss called me in to give me the great news that he wanted me to work on about four or five additional tasks. I remained calm, but my level of enthusiasm definitely was not aligned with his. I cried on the way home, so frustrated that I had no idea how I was going to make this work. I went to bed early in hopes of more mental clarity in the morning. Over the weekend, I sat outside in the sun with my thoughts just trying to figure out how to approach this. I went for a run and tried to get myself out of a growing state of anxiety. That's when inspiration struck.

I came back and documented my creative strategy and the feedback I was going to provide to my boss the following Monday. It was risky, and I knew it might backfire. He might not be as impressed with my "creative genius" as I was in that current moment, but he was an open-minded person who seemed to not be threatened by honest feedback, and I thought he would ultimately appreciate it. So, on Monday morning, I asked him to come to the break room sink with me. I got out a cup and handed him a piece of paper and began to fill the cup as I spoke:

1. This is an employee working at full Capacity. [Cup filled with water at about 80 percent] The cup is not full because slack is needed. Slack allows for . . .
2. Unexpected opportunities . . . unplanned issues . . . unforeseen circumstances . . . acts of God . . . bumps in the road . . . illness . . . delays . . . supply chain issues. Now the cup is full—to the top! [Cup filled with water completely to the top]
3. When you are working at capacity and continue to add items onto people, without regard to capacity and slack, the result is spillover. [Water running into cup and cup overflowing]

Spillover = stress, anxiety, lower quality, dropped balls, unfinished projects, poor client experience, lower employee engagement, emotional situations

When we better understand Capacity, Slack, and Spillover, we are better able to accomplish the organization's goals with as little despair as possible.

We were able to have a very candid discussion about all that I was working on and how I couldn't take on anything else unless I stopped doing my current tasks. He was very receptive and apologetic, and he appreciated the way I had gone about making the situation so clear and objective.

I share this to show that at some point, everyone needs feedback. Think about how you can provide that critical feedback in a productive and positive manner to whomever may need it.

• • • • •

Radical Candor is the healthy way to communicate, coach, and lead your team. It's up to YOU as the leader to set the example and guide people along this path. It's not easy at all. You will feel a lot of discomfort. But you will help your team be more caring, more authentic, more real, and more productive. Unicorn Leaders take steps to lead with compassion, genuinely care for their team members (including their boss), and provide them with candid feedback to help ensure you are able to achieve amazing results together.

UNICORN LEADER ACTION STEPS

- Watch the videos at www.radicalcandor.com/resources to get an excellent understanding of the framework. You will receive a great overview in just six minutes or get even more detail in thirty minutes.
- Watch the interview of Alan Mulally on *Jay Leno's Garage* for leadership inspiration: www.youtube.com/watch?v=u4aatqMxFnE.

CHAPTER SEVEN

Employee Engagement

We either make ourselves miserable or we make ourselves strong. The amount of work is the same. —CARLOS CASTANEDA

Only 15 percent of the world's employees are engaged at work or have a "great job," according to Gallup research. A "great job" is full-time work, a living-wage paycheck, and the ability to do meaningful and fulfilling work, and it fosters individual growth and development. People with great jobs have better life outcomes. These engaged employees help grow your business, inspire teams, solve problems, volunteer in their community, and have better health and well-being. What is tragic is the rest of the world's employees (85 percent of people) are either just going through the motions or actually hate their jobs, managers, and companies. Their jobs have no meaning and therefore, sadly, neither do their lives. We need to become aware of what leads to disengagement and how we can prevent it for ourselves and those we lead.

SUNDAY SICKNESS

Do you know what Sunday Sickness is? Unfortunately, I bet you do. It's that sick feeling you start to get on Sunday afternoon or evening when you realize tomorrow is Monday and you have to go back to work. Sunday Sickness is that sense of dread you have when you contemplate Monday. It's that gnawing feeling of despair or depression. It's what causes you to be sure to stop to buy a lottery ticket . . . or maybe have just one more drink to numb the anxiety that the thought of Monday causes you. Why do we feel that way? How can we take steps to avoid it and honestly not dread Monday?

I don't remember when or where I actually heard this phrase, but I know I've been aware of this unfortunate phenomenon for over twenty years. I have been on a personal mission to avoid this sickness myself and help ensure my team members avoid it.

For many years, I have intentionally monitored how I feel on Sunday afternoons. Do I feel dread? Concern? Despair? Anxiety? Or maybe . . . not much of anything? Even better, do I feel anticipation? Eagerness? General happiness? Positivity? I can tell you that when I have the opportunity to be in a role that allows me to use my strengths, add value, and feel valued, then I feel no concern of Monday approaching. I may even be a bit excited to see the day come and get back to work on items I love. I am very grateful for those times in life. I know how valuable these feelings are, and I feel fortunate that I have mostly been in roles like that. I have had two very specific times in my life where I had an extremely bad case of Sunday Sickness.

The first time, I was in my thirties and in a role that was spinning in circles due to the indecisiveness, or lack of buy-in, from the top and across the organization. I basically had to request to be off on the weekends. Yes, you heard that correctly: request to be off on Saturday and Sunday! It was rare that we actually ever had to work on weekends, but we had to be "on call" or prepared to work "just in case." And during the week, not much was accomplished. It was so obvious that a project named "Get it Done" was renamed to "[Never Going to] Get it Done." This position was deeply unfulfilling and went against all my strengths (Achiever, Competition, Focus, Learner, Significance), and it was soul-sucking. So I took steps to find another job, and I did.

The next time, I was in my forties, and it was a similar situation of spinning in circles, who's on first, what are we doing, where are we going, do this—no! Do that. I recognized that sick feeling for quite a while and knew it was time to go. This time when it happened, I had also been preaching the concept of Sunday Sickness Avoidance to my team for years! It was evident that what I had been telling them to be sure to watch out for and avoid had gotten to me. Not only did I need to leave for myself and my own well-being, I needed to leave for them. It was important to set the example and walk the talk.

It's crucial to be aware of Sunday sickness. When you first start to notice this feeling, it's time to take action. If you happen to have a leader who is receptive, I encourage you to reach out and talk to them about your feelings and perhaps determine what strengths aren't being utilized. Perhaps you can work it out together and get yourself in a better situation that doesn't make you sick on Sundays.

But if not, make note. Draw a line in the sand of how long you will tolerate this feeling. For me, it has always been one year. So much can change in a year. I think it is very important to give the universe time to work things out, one way or another. But after a year of almost every Sunday being filled with dread about Monday, it's paramount to take steps and move on. Maybe it's time to put on AJR's song "BANG!"—and accept that it may have "been a hell of a ride but I'm thinking it's time to go."

LIFE IS TOO SHORT TO HATE YOUR JOB

Life is just too short. Don't waste your time dreading Mondays and being sick on Sundays. You have only one life, but there are many jobs to choose from out there. What if you found out you had only six months to live? What regrets would you have? You would probably regret time wasted feeling anxious. You would probably regret you didn't (or couldn't) make the most of your Sundays because you were dreading Monday.

If you are just trying to "get through" Monday through Friday, that is no way to live. I once wrote in my journal: "I'm tired of just getting through things." And I swear, later that week, my boss kept talking about how we just had to "get through" this and "get through" that. And my entire being thought, *No!* If we are just getting through everything, there is no joy, no growth, no love in what you are doing. Life is just too short for that.

However, realizing this and doing something about it are two different things. You must take intentional steps to live the life you want. I can't tell you how many times I've had to distance myself from people who just want to sit around and complain about their job, their life, or their situation. As Bozoma Saint John has said, "We spend far too much time complaining about the way things are and forget that we have the power to change anything and everything." Yes! But you have to take ***intentional*** steps to do so.

I once had a friend who had not only Sunday sickness but Monday-Saturday sickness. She also had six million dollars in the bank. I kept telling her, "Just leave. Life's too short to hate your job. Walk away." But she wouldn't (couldn't) do it until she found another job. We all have to make our own choices, and only we know what we can live with or where our boundaries are. I would encourage you to not waste a single moment of your life—especially if you have six million dollars!

I read a life-changing article once by Tim Urban called "Your Life in Weeks." The article discusses how sometimes life seems really short and other times it seems impossibly long, but really life is "most certainly finite." It illustrated a human life of ninety years broken down by weeks—and those are the only weeks you've got. These precious weeks of your life should be filled with a combination of enjoyment and improving your life/the lives of others. If you are doing neither of those things, you become depressed, frustrated, and hopeless. This is no way to live!

As part of the article, there is a Life Calendar you can purchase. This calendar lays out every week of your life in boxes on one sheet of paper (assuming you live to be ninety). I have one on my wall. As part of my fiftieth birthday journey, I colored in every box that I had lived up until that point. It was a great way to reflect on my life and remember all the great times, as well as all the really bad times. It reminded me of all I have overcome and accomplished. It reminded me of good friends, wonderful family, amazing trips—and also of big mistakes, terrible pain, and points of failure. But mostly, it provided a tangible reminder that all the remaining empty and not-yet-colored-in boxes are mine to fill up. Those remaining boxes can be whatever I want them to be! I can choose how I spend my time and what I do with those remaining weeks of my life. I can choose to not be sick on Sunday. I can choose to not hate Monday-Friday.

Please repeat along with me: Life is too short to hate your job!

THE SIGNS OF A MISERABLE JOB

According to Patrick Lencioni, there are three signs of a miserable job:

1. No one knows who you are.
2. Your efforts don't seem to matter.
3. You have no idea if you are heading in the right direction.

People who are miserable in their jobs dread going to work and come home frustrated and depressed. They are exhausted and find themselves becoming cynical. The soul-sucking misery of a miserable job erodes self-confidence and passion. I had a miserable job once, and here are some of my journal entries from that time:

I feel so sad and unworthy . . . so depressed and overwhelmed . . . I just want to quit my job—everything is so annoying and disjointed . . . broken, gutted, unmotivated . . . so tired, so unmotivated, dreading this week . . . self-doubt, no self-worth, working through it . . . survived another week . . . I can't sleep, I can't cry.

The impact that a miserable job has on a person's life is real. Leaders need take action to assess their workplace, to rid it of soul-sucking misery and take steps to ensure the jobs are not miserable. What are some steps you can take?

- **Get to know your employees**. Employees need to be understood and appreciated for their unique qualities. Provide attention and care for your team members. Help people love their jobs. Get to know each one of your team members and what makes them special. Talk about their strengths and the value they bring to the team. Discuss their goals and what they would like to achieve. Understand what they are going through professionally and personally; be available to assist as you can.
- **Help employees see their work has purpose**. Help your team connect the dots and see how their work makes a difference. Having a purpose encourages people get out of bed in the morning and helps them have a sense of fulfilment at the end of the day. Help your team members see the value they bring to you, the team, and the overall organization.
- **Show employees progress toward goals**. Articulate goals and regularly share a progress report. Employees need to have a tangible way to measure progress. Use a poster, a PowerPoint, or a dashboard—just be sure to show them where you are and where you are going. Team members need to know what the expectations are so they can contribute and help control their destiny. Regularly discuss goals, obstacles, and results with your team.

Unicorn Leaders realize job (and life) misery is unnecessary and can be course-corrected. There are real and actionable things you can do as a leader to prevent job misery. Take proactive steps each day to prevent misery—and instead, provide joy. When you have great leaders who can maximize the potential of every team member, you have the ability to provide yourself and others with a great job and a great life!

Please say it with me again: Life is too short to hate your job!

SAVE YOUR MONEY

It's important to save your money. Not just for retirement, a new car, or a vacation. It's important to save your money for FREEDOM. A friend's grandmother always told her, "If you are always ready, you never have to get ready." I love that. I'm a planner, so I know I'm always working on being ready every single day. Are you?

Entrepreneur and author Gary Vaynerchuk has asked, "Why are you spending money on stuff you don't need to impress people you don't like?" I love that! Do you need that new car to drive to a soul-sucking job that is causing you dread and despair?

My mom always said, "If you spend everything you make, you will never have anything." Seems like a pretty simple concept, but why do so many people do just that and live paycheck to paycheck? Life is too short. Stop it!

If you can miss some paychecks and still pay your bills and feed your family, you have the power to change your life. You have the power to walk away from despair and desperation and find a better situation. You don't have to put up with a boss who says you are stupid or ignores you for a year. You can quit a job you hate and build a life you love. Save your money and empower your soul.

One more time . . . please say it with me: Life is too short to hate your job!

As employees, we deserve not to have a miserable job. As leaders, we owe it to our team members to do everything in our power to ensure their job is not miserable. Let's take intentional steps to increase employee engagement. Let's be more mindful of how we are spending our days and our lives. Save your money! Every day, in every way, Unicorn Leaders remember that life is just too short and there are things we can do to help ensure the days we are given are filled with more joy than misery.

UNICORN LEADER ACTION STEPS

- Read Tim Urban's article "Your Life in Weeks": www.waitbutwhy.com/2014/05/life-weeks.html. Consider purchasing his Life Calendar and becoming more intentional about how you are filling up the "boxes" of your life.
- Read the book *The Truth about Employee Engagement: A Fable about Addressing the Three Root Causes of Job Misery* by Patrick Lencioni and take steps to ensure your team members do not have a miserable job.

CHAPTER EIGHT

Mental Toughness

You have power over your mind not outside events. Realize this, and you will find strength. —MARCUS AURELIUS

To achieve high performance, we must learn how to build emotional strength and resilience. Being able to thrive in challenging situations and using these challenges to become a better leader is critical. This takes awareness and a lot of work. By taking intentional steps to get stronger, we become better equipped to manage and overcome setbacks and frustrations. When we improve our physical, emotional, mental, and spiritual capacity, we improve our ability to perform and lead. We can train ourselves to find the calm in chaos and choose more productive responses to circumstances in our life.

BECOME STRONGER

There was a point in my career when I became aware that I needed to improve my mental toughness to achieve the results I desired. I had reached my goal of becoming an "executive" and couldn't understand why I didn't find the executive life as exciting and rewarding as I had always hoped. More and more, I found the experience frustrating and unfulfilling because I was spending my days dealing with corporate politics, overall dysfunction, and some very toxic situations. I began to believe I wasn't cut out to be an executive because I didn't seem to be dealing with this very well. I felt most of my days were wasted on stroking egos and tap dancing around conflict. I was becoming emotional and overwhelmed. I told a friend that, to survive, I had to "put my heart in a jar on a shelf." I wrote "work harder, nobody cares" on my whiteboard.

As the days passed and I reread my whiteboard statement, I knew I needed to do something. This wasn't the attitude I wanted in my life. I researched and began to read articles and books on mental toughness. Finding myself an executive coach became important. I was on a mission to toughen up and gain the strength to survive and thrive at the top.

One of my favorite articles on this topic is "The Making of a Corporate Athlete" by Jim Loehr and Tony Schwartz. In this article, they illustrate the various levels of performance with a High-Performance Pyramid. The pyramid builds on the rituals that are required at each level. The theory is that to achieve Ideal Performance State (performance under pressure), you must get all levels working together. You must combine rituals in the following areas to reach the highest levels of performance: physical, emotional, mental, and spiritual. I encourage you to read the article in its entirety for additional insight and guidance.

We all know we "should" eat healthy, get proper sleep, and exercise regularly, but sometimes we neglect to do these things, and it catches up with us. We have to start with the basics and build a strong foundation if we ever hope to improve. I know that when I am running, sleeping, and eating well on a consistent basis, my "foundation" is strong and gives me the ability to optimize my emotional, mental, and spiritual capacity.

Becoming more aware of the state of your emotional capacity is critical. When I "put my heart in a jar on a shelf," it was because I was letting negative emotions get the best of me. All the frustration, sadness, fear, and anger of the situation was draining my energy and taking away my positive vibes. Exercise can help with both physical and emotional capacity. Feeling frustrated? Sad or mad? Give yourself thirty minutes to just take a break. Go for a run. Take a walk. Listen to some upbeat and inspiring music.

Music can lift us up, improve our mood, and adjust our attitude. Some of my go-to songs that help make me feel stronger and inspire me to get through challenging circumstances are:

- "The Show Must Go On" by Queen
- "Hang Tough" by Tesla
- "Whatever It Takes" by Imagine Dragons
- "Stronger" by Britney Spears
- "Victorious" by Panic at the Disco
- "No Easy Way Out" by Robert Tepper

(Yes, I have eclectic tastes.) What are some of your favorite songs of inspiration? Play them! Let those songs feed your soul and keep you going.

Another thing that can help is getting your body and mind to a place of calm. Installing the Calm app on my phone was invaluable. I always do a brief meditation prior to a meeting or interaction with certain people who seemed to increase my level of anxiety or frustration. Meditation has been shown to provide us with mental renewal and improved emotional and mental capacity. Take some time to sit still, breathe, and do nothing for ten minutes.

Finally, tapping into your values and personal sense of purpose can improve your spiritual capacity. Write in a journal, focus on gratitude, and serve others. These activities can help shift your mindset and provide an important break from constant goal-oriented activity.

When I began to learn more about how the physical, emotional, mental, and spiritual aspects all work together, I realized what I had written on my white board—"work harder, no one cares"—was a flawed approach and not the way to achieve overall excellence.

BE AWARE OF TRIGGERS

My executive coach introduced me to the book *Triggers: Creating Behavior That Lasts—Becoming the Person You Want to Be* by Marshall Goldsmith. A trigger is any stimulus that impacts our behavior. When we become aware of various triggers in our life and how we can learn to better respond to them, we can have more control of the consequences. I'm so grateful for Marshall Goldsmith's insight and learning the many concepts he discusses in this book. One of these concepts is "AIWATT," and this can be life changing if you apply it:

> **A**m **I** **w**illing
> **a**t **t**his **t**ime,
> to make the investment required
> to make a positive difference
> on this topic?

We have a choice every day, in every situation, to either engage or "let it go." Our life situations tempt us to engage in time-wasting situations. Inconsequential things cause us anxiety, stress, loss of sleep, and unhappiness. Once you realize and embrace the fact that you don't have to react—you can literally do nothing—it is freeing. By really empowering yourself in this way, you can be on the way to becoming the person you want to be.

Similar to this, is the Buddhist wisdom found in "The Empty Boat" by Chuang Tzu. This basically points out that if you are crossing a river and an empty boat hits your boat, you will not shout or become angry. But if you see that there is a person in the boat—suddenly you are angry and shouting.

The important lesson to always remember: *There's never anyone in the other boat.* When we get mad, or enraged, or upset at people or situations, we are simply punishing ourselves. An empty boat is not out to get us and neither are the people creating stress and anxiety in our lives. They are just being who they are, and we are choosing to let them drive us crazy and allowing them to make us unhappy. Stop it! See them for the empty boats they are. Let. It. Go.

When you embrace AIWATT and understand "The Empty Boat," you can more easily determine whether a battle is worth fighting. You can decide whether you are allowing others to control your emotions, your reactions, and your consequences. Take the time to breathe and ask yourself why in the world you would empower someone else with control over your life. It's yours. Control your emotions. Control your reactions. Control your life.

Awareness is the first step. Practice is the next. Continued focus and learning makes us better.

I knew about AIWATT and "The Empty Boat," but then a storm came along and tested whether I could put it into practice. There was so much disruption, confusion, and frustration happening at work. A certain empty boat came my way, and I yelled at it, kicked it, and punished myself. But the good news was I recognized I had just failed a test. So I dug a little deeper and found another wonderful resource in the book *The Stoic Challenge: A Philosopher's Guide to Becoming Tougher, Calmer, and More Resilient* by William B. Irvine. Here are some highlights:

- Think of setbacks as a test of your character. Alter your emotional response to them. Develop your ability to stay calm.
- When faced with a setback, treat it as a test of your resilience and resourcefulness, devised and administered by imaginary Stoic gods whose goal is throwing curveballs our way to make our days not harder but better.
- Setbacks are not to punish us but to give us an opportunity to do something courageous and thereby increase our chances of attaining the highest possible excellence.

All are wonderful nuggets of advice and give us an excellent perspective. Adjust your mindset. It's a test. A point in time. An irritant to make us stronger, to teach us a valuable lesson, to help us achieve excellence. Adjust your emotional response and reaction accordingly, and you will be victorious. It's important to remember that we can't control the events in our life, but we can control our response.

I have found much success in combining these thoughts with the foundation of exercise. When I run, I think about any current frustrating situations and frame them as a test or an opportunity. I run and work through in my mind how I can rise up and accept the challenge of a difficult or seemingly hopeless situation and become the victor, not the victim. Teach yourself to turn adversity into an overall training exercise on the road to greatness.

DO MORE OF WHAT YOU LOVE

Now, let's examine "work/life balance." This is a concept I never bought into or experienced, because I have never had balance. Especially since I became a working mom, I've always felt like I'm on a roller coaster without a seat belt trying to hold on and juggle knives at the same time. I know it sounds like a bad thing, but it really hasn't been (most of the time). When I read *Nine Lies About Work: A Freethinking Leader's Guide to the Real World* by Marcus Buckingham and Ashley Goodall, it brought such clarity!

"Neither you nor your life are in balance, nor will you ever be. Instead, you are a unique creature who takes inputs from the world, metabolizes them in some way, produces something useful, and does so in such a way that you can keep doing it."

It is very important to love what you do and do what you love.

When you are "in love" with your work, you are more productive, energetic, creative, joyful, resilient, and strong. You flourish. You are excited. You look forward to it. You enjoy the moments you are doing it. You can't wait to do it again. You dramatically lower the risk of burnout. Pay attention to what you love to do. Spend some time really analyzing what you look forward to doing, when time seems to fly and what you can't wait to do again. Then, find a way to do more of this!

Take intentional steps to do more of what you love. You won't find balance, but you will find more love and joy in your life.

My friend and coach, Apryl Schlueter, provided inspiration on the topic of work-life balance in her book *Finding Success in Balance: My Journey to the Cheerful Mind*. She provides excellent tips and perspective, and she encourages us to find a healthy balance among family, career, relationships, and more while reminding us that "balance" means different things to different people. How do you know whether you have a healthy balance? You regularly self-assess and determine whether you feel overwhelmed, stressed out, and generally dissatisfied. Take time to reflect on what adjustments can be made in all the areas of your life that might help bring you more peace and happiness.

INSPIRATION

One source of inspiration for me is to learn from super-successful people. I particularly like successful people who have a splash of crazy, and one of those that I follow is Jesse Itzler. One year, in the month of February, he ran the number of miles per day that corresponded with the day of the month. So, on February 1, he ran one mile . . . on February 15, he ran fifteen miles . . . on February 28, he ran twenty-eight miles. Every single day, he ran. One mile, then two, then three, and so on! Has anyone else ever tried that? I know I haven't, but that is so inspiring to me!

I was first introduced to the inspiring craziness of Jesse in his book *Living with a Seal: 31 Days Training with the Toughest Man on the Planet*. It documents the thirty-one days he brought a Navy Seal into his home to train him and toughen him up. This particular Navy Seal is widely considered to be the toughest athlete on the planet. The book is hilarious and awe-inspiring and filled with many good lessons. The Seal tells us "Every day, do something that makes you uncomfortable," and reminds us "You can always keep going." The Seal pushed Jesse to work out every single day. One day, the workout was running 16 miles and doing 700 pushups; another day, it was 17 miles with 5.5 miles of it in a 50-pound vest. Raining, snowing, freezing—it didn't matter. The Seal would say, "If you think it's fourteen degrees, then it's fourteen degrees. Personally, I'm looking at it like it's in the mid-fifties."

The Seal focused on the discipline needed to control the mind and embrace the pain. He would say, "The tougher the conditions, the more I like my odds." That is so powerful!

• • • • •

A Unicorn Leader will learn to become more resilient. Train yourself to have physical, emotional, mental, and spiritual strength so you can be the very best you can be. Take care of yourself and ensure you are getting the right amount of healthy food, exercise, and sleep. Listen to music. Breathe. Learn techniques from others to help ensure you are performing at peak capacity. Find inspiration. Become more mentally tough, and you will improve your ability to lead both yourself and others.

UNICORN LEADER ACTION STEPS

- Spend ten minutes doing nothing. Breathe in and breathe out. Think about what you are grateful for in your life. Think about your happiest memory from childhood or your favorite vacation spot. Just enjoy this moment of silence and calm. Focus on your source of spirituality.
- Go for a walk or a run. Build up your physical stamina. Lift some weights. Join an exercise class. Work on getting stronger physically, emotionally, and mentally.

CHAPTER NINE

Perspective

What you see and what you hear depends a great deal on where you are standing.

—C. S. LEWIS

Being able to see another person's point of view is critical in leadership and in life. Very few are able to appreciate another human's perspective unless they have walked a mile in their shoes, as the saying goes. When we contemplate certain scenarios and are curious about the circumstances of others' lives, we open ourselves up to another level of understanding. Taking steps to improve our emotional intelligence and our self-awareness is very powerful and can dramatically improve our ability to lead.

HAVE YOU EVER . . .

Have you ever been a working mom? If not, then you probably don't understand the stress they are under in the workplace and how much anxiety is created when they see a call from the school or daycare coming across their phone. First thought, *What has happened to my child*? Next immediate thought, *How will this impact the rest of my day and what issues will it cause when I have to leave?* If you work for a great boss who trusts you and understands these things happen, or perhaps is a working mom and can totally relate, then your anxiety level probably doesn't reach maximum levels. Also, if you are a salaried employee, are able to work remotely, and have some general flexibility, you probably have lower anxiety levels. But if you are an hourly employee with a terrible boss who has no perspective, I can't even imagine the anxiety that results from this situation. Especially if you are a SINGLE working mom.

How about a dual-income household with children? Similar anxiety levels, depending on the level of equality in your household. On top of anxiety, you must also juggle/negotiate/agree with the other person and determine who can leave work now, who will suffer the least consequence for doing so, etc. Along with work stress, you now have relationship stress. The amount of overall stress increases if you BOTH have bosses with no perspective or empathy for your situation.

In your adult life, have you ever made $20,000 or less? How about $50,000 or less? If so, then you know any impact to your paycheck has a huge impact on your life. You also know it's more challenging to save as much as you would like. To save anything at all, it's necessary to sacrifice a lot every day and have a string of good luck so you don't have to dip into that savings. You also realize you must put up with a lot of terrible bosses and stressful situations to survive.

I could go on and on with "have you ever" scenarios, but the point is this: many leaders have not experienced any of this. Unless they are very insightful and connected to the human experience, they simply don't get it. That is how we end up with terrible HR policies and unfortunate workplace decisions, ultimately creating additional unnecessary stress for employees. Perhaps you have always received a salary of at least $75,000 (which research indicates is where the relationship between happiness and income plateaus, according to Daniel Kahneman and Angus Deaton), and so your perspective may be a bit skewed.

Take this quick quiz to determine your perspective:

1. One of your best employees continues to leave work to pick up their sick child from school. Even though they have left work unexpectedly once a week or more for the past several weeks, they have completed the necessary work and have not missed any deadlines. They are very apologetic and have recently told you their son has chronic strep and no matter what antibiotic is used, the doctor cannot seem to get it cured.

   Do you:

   A. Tell them to be sure and log any hours missed as PTO/Sick Time/Unpaid and that you expect this situation to not impact any future deadlines

   B. Thank them for letting you know, tell them how impressed you are that they have been able to juggle a sick child with work demands, and ask how you can help

2. A historic winter storm affects your organization and as a result, many of your employees are without power and water. Additionally, many have school closures, elderly family member issues, and other concerns to deal with. The road conditions and property management issues are so bad, your organization decides to close many locations. For the locations that remain open, you require those team members to risk their safety and drive there as quickly as possible. Your employees work if they can, continuing to balance personal constraints and work demands to the best of their ability.

   Do you:

   A. Decide that anyone who wasn't able to work during this storm (due to acts of God or based on decisions made by the company) must take PTO and feel the best way to convey this decision is with a company-wide email.

B. Decide to pay everyone as if they worked full-time during that time period because you know that IF they were able, they were working; and IF they weren't able, it was largely out of their control. You understand the stress and anxiety the situation has caused them, and you want to help support them during this stressful time

If you selected A, I'm guessing it's mostly because of lack of perspective.

For question #1, YOU have never had the stress of trying to juggle extreme family issues with work demands. YOU are probably not a single mom or a dual-income family member with children, and you aren't making less than $50,000.

For question #2, YOU were not personally impacted. YOU could work comfortably from home (or maybe even your second home). YOU did not have to drive in dangerous conditions. YOU were not personally dealing with a combination of family, work, safety, and other issues all at one time.

If you selected B, I belive you are on the path to becoming a Unicorn Leader.

CHECK YOURSELF

Having perspective also requires leaders to constantly check themselves. Maybe it's been a while since you made less than $75,000 and were a working parent. Since then, you've been successful and now are very high up in the corporate food chain, enjoying flexibility and control. Don't let your current fortunate situation cloud your perspective. Chances are many people working in your organization don't make as much as you, don't have some of the luxuries that you enjoy, and can't relate to your current lifestyle.

Once, I was invited to attend a welcome lunch with a couple of critical new employees I had hired. I was proud that my company and the other attendees recognized the arrival of these two new leaders as so important that they would prioritize their time this way. Providing a nice lunch, and time with executive leadership as one of the first experiences they would have with me, was very rewarding. The lunch started off with pleasant conversation and delicious bread, but soon took a wrong turn. The executive conversation quickly turned away from focusing on the new employees, getting to know them, and helping them to better know the company to discussions on Rolexes, art collections, second homes, and luxury vacations. I was horrified and couldn't wait for the lunch to be over. The new leaders remained gracious and as engaged as possible, but it was unfortunate that such a potentially positive experience had gone so astray due to the lack of perspective of executives who had clearly lost touch.

Please note: most people do not have two or three houses. It is embarrassing for them and you to try to have discussions along these lines. What might be more effective and appreciated is to tell your story of how you achieved the success you have so far, share any lessons you learned along the way, and provide acknowledgement to those who helped you get where you are. Having perspective means having some self-awareness. Without perspective and self-awareness, you simply cannot be a Unicorn Leader.

EMOTIONAL INTELLIGENCE

What do you need to be a great leader? A high IQ? Superior technical skills? According to Daniel Goleman, it is neither of those. In his book *Social Intelligence,* he explains that there are a group of five skills that enable the best leaders to maximize performance: self-awareness, self-regulation, motivation, empathy, and social skill.

Most people are controlled by their emotions. As humans, we are emotional creatures, so our first reaction will likely be emotional. Many people have not taken the time to recognize their emotions and use them in a beneficial way. We go along in our life feeling either happiness, sadness, anger, fear, or shame throughout our days to various levels of intensity. But how we respond and react to an emotion is within our control—as long as we are aware. Emotional intelligence is our ability to recognize and understand emotions in ourselves and others and our ability to use this awareness to manage our behavior and relationships . . . and ultimately determine our success in life.

Research shows that when star performers are compared with average performers in senior leadership positions, the difference was related to emotional intelligence factors. The great news is emotional intelligence can be improved through practice and feedback. You can take action to become a star performer. This is exciting news for anyone on the journey to becoming a Unicorn Leader!

Your IQ (intelligence quotient) is your ability to learn and is the same at any age. Your EQ (emotional quotient) can be improved and developed over the course of your life. This is great news, because every point increase in EQ adds $1,300 to an annual salary, according to Travis Bradberry and Jean Greaves in the book *Emotional Intelligence 2.0*. Any of us can take steps at any time to improve and become a better leader. Take steps to break old behavioral habits and establish new ones. Enlist the help of an executive coach, a life coach, or a counselor to assist you in this journey. Seek feedback from your boss, your peers, and your employees and focus on areas of weakness. Improving emotional intelligence takes genuine desire and effort, but it can be done.

SELF-AWARENESS

Self-awareness is the ability to recognize your own emotions and is perhaps the most critical of the emotional intelligence competencies. When you are self-aware, you are better able to stay in control of your reactions to events, challenges, and people. When you understand your emotional tendencies, you can make better sense of your emotions. Self-awareness is like a superpower! According to findings in the book *Emotional Intelligence 2.0*, people with high self-awareness are very clear in their understanding of what they do well, what motivates and satisfies them, and which people and situations push their buttons.

In her book *Insight: The Surprising Truth About How Others See Us, How We See Ourselves, and Why the Answers Matter More Than We Think,* Dr. Tasha Eurich explains: "Self-awareness is the meta-skill of the twenty-first century. The qualities most critical for success in today's world such as empathy, communication, and collaboration, all stem from self-awareness. The more self-aware we are, the better able we are to be strong team players and exceptional leaders. As self-awareness increases, people's satisfaction with their life increases. They are more likely to pursue the right opportunities, put their strengths to work and keep emotions from holding them back. It's important to note that 83% of people high in self-awareness are top performers."

A terrifying bit of research shows that the *least* competent people are usually the *most* confident in their abilities. You probably know someone like that—just make very sure it isn't YOU!

Self-awareness is skill you can improve. You can take steps to become a "self-awareness unicorn"—people who have made transformational improvements in their self-awareness, according to Dr. Tasha Eurich. These unicorns have two things in common: a belief in the supreme importance of self-awareness and a commitment to develop it throughout their lives.

To become this type of unicorn, it's important we take steps to work on both internal self-awareness and external self-awareness.

- Internal self-awareness: understanding of your values, passions, aspirations, reactions, and impact on others
- External self-awareness: knowing how others see you

There are many ways to work on these areas, including determining your level of narcissism and your level of humility, and proactively seeking honest and objective feedback. It's hard work—I'm not going to lie to you. I spent a good deal of time in 2020 working my way through the Insight Course (theinsightcourse.com). I would recommend it to anyone who is serious about improving self-awareness and wants to become a unicorn.

PSYCHOPATHS AND NARCISSISTS

Do you think that your boss might be a psychopath? According to Stephanie Sarkis, you might be on to something. About one percent of the population may qualify as having psychopathic behavior, while among senior executives, that rate climbs to 3.5 percent.

In her article "Senior Executives are More Likely to be Psychopaths," she writes "Psychopathic behavior is marked by knowing right from wrong, but engaging in immoral and illegal behavior anyway; sabotaging others, pitting people against each other and manipulating others; displaying 'cognitive empathy,' but not true empathy; having a facade of charisma, engaging in criminal activities and lacking remorse for behavior." Do you know anyone like that?

As Jack McCollough reported in his January 2020 Forbes article, "Roughly 4% to as high as 12% of CEOs exhibit psychopathic traits . . . more in line with the 15% rate found in prisons." Psychopaths are generally considered intelligent, manipulative, and charming—and lack the ability to learn from mistakes or punishment. Some are quick to anger, though when climbing the corporate ladder, they are more likely to use charm and flattery on superiors in order to propel their careers.

Narcissists aren't quite as dangerous as psychopaths but can definitely do a lot of damage to the people around them. They have a grandiose sense of self-importance and lack empathy. It is all about them, and they need your adoration. They tend to be highly competitive and readily exploit the people in their lives. They don't like to be questioned or challenged.

I have definitely worked with individuals who have these tendencies. I knew of a CEO that refused to wait in line. He would go to the front of any line he encountered and demand to be seated or served. He was much too important to wait in line! I knew of another CEO who repeatedly mentioned how lucky we were that he had arrived to save the company. He had no interest in learning any history behind decisions that had been made or gaining any perspective on the situation. He was clearly smarter than everyone in the room!

Have you ever worked with or for someone like this?

Unfortunately, at some point in your life, you will probably either associate with, work alongside, or work for a psychopath or narcissist. The quicker you identify these individuals for what they are as a result of their behavior, the greater your chances of avoiding being victimized.

In our journey to increase our self-awareness, it's important to be aware of the self-centered culture we now live in and determine how caught up in it we may be. How many selfies do you post in a day or in a week? Narcissism is on the rise in a world filled with constant social media posts.

Do you have narcissistic qualities? There is a quick quiz you can do to find out. The appendix of *Insight: The Surprising Truth About How Others See Us, How We See Ourselves, and Why the Answers Matter More Than We Think* by Dr. Tasha Eurich provides several examples to choose from, such as:

- I always know what I am doing vs. Sometimes I am not sure of what I'm doing
- I am an extraordinary person vs. I am much like everybody else

This exercise can help determine whether you have some work to do to resist narcissistic behavior and improve your overall self-awareness.

I am saddened to admit I have some narcissistic qualities. Perhaps it is because I was a spoiled only child . . . perhaps it is a trait within my overall personality . . . perhaps a combination of both of these reasons and so many other variables. Who knows? The good news is I am AWARE of this, which is the first step in resisting narcissistic actions and will propel me further in my overall journey toward improved self-awareness.

• • • • •

Open your mind and consider another perspective. Look at situations from another point of view. Consider the fact that how you see the world may not be how others see it. Take action today to improve your emotional intelligence and self-awareness so you can be the best Unicorn Leader (and person) you can be.

UNICORN LEADER ACTION STEPS

- Take an EQ assessment. There is a quick and free one at www.mindtools.com, or for a more in-depth option, I recommend the *Emotional Intelligence 2.0* book and assessment available at www.talentsmarteq.com/test/. Start improving your EQ today so you can be an exceptional leader tomorrow!
- Take the Insight Quiz at www.tashaeurich.com and use other resources on the website to learn more about improving your self-awareness. Put in the work and begin your self-awareness journey today! Commit to the action necessary to see yourself more clearly and become the very best you can be.

CHAPTER TEN

Relationships

All good leadership is based on relationships.
—JOHN MAXWELL

It's critical in life to build relationships. Every day, people are at the core of our life. The better we are at getting along, forming friendships, and really connecting with others, the more successful we will be at our career and in life. Building our credibility helps to build our influence. By having a genuine interest in helping others, we will reap many rewards along the way. Taking the time to reach out, learn from, and show appreciation for the unique human beings that cross our paths will truly enrich our journey.

GETTING ALONG WITH PEOPLE

How to Win Friends and Influence People was one of the very first "business" books I read. I was in my early twenties, and it was life-changing. In my young life, I had not had much direct exposure to these concepts. I hadn't really experienced many people with great communication and people skills. To read these stories about ways to make people like you and how to win people to your way of thinking was truly enlightening. I gained a lot of insight on what I could do differently. I learned how I could improve myself going forward. The principles explained throughout the book helped build a foundation of how to improve my ability to get along with people early in my career.

Some of the principles according to Dale Carnegie include:

- Don't criticize, condemn, or complain
- Become genuinely interested in people
- Smile
- Give honest and sincere appreciation
- Try honestly to see things from the other person's point of view

Very basic and simple but so useful and relevant. Very often in life, the simplest concepts can be the most powerful. That is certainly true in this case. We have the opportunity to use these principles every day. When we build on these basic people skills, we can achieve great success and happiness.

BUILD RELATIONSHIPS AND INFLUENCE

While conducting an interview, I asked the candidate to tell me her favorite business book. She responded, "*The 360 Degree Leader* by John Maxwell." It was a book I had not yet read, so I ordered it that day and read it soon thereafter. One of the important reminders from this book is "It's more important to get along with people than to get ahead of them. If you make it your goal to reach out to others and build relationships with them, you will derive fulfillment wherever you are."

This was very consistent with Dale Carnegie's wisdom, and it helped me build on those early principles.

The 360 Degree Leader is mindful about developing their influence from anywhere in the organization. You must deliver outstanding performance and be someone who can be counted on by various people and various levels.

As John Maxwell tells us: "Every day we must work on our ability to lead up, across, and down. We need to proactively reach out across the organization to develop relationships. We must find out what we can learn from various individuals and determine what we can do to help them be more successful." Take time to ask your boss, your direct reports, your peers, and your colleagues "What can I do to help?" And be willing to actually do it.

This is so powerful and so consistent with what I believe a Unicorn Leader really is. Being there for others and having a genuine desire to help them is a critical desire of any Unicorn Leader.

It's important to build your reputation as a person who can "get $hit done" with all these groups. Find a way to make things happen. Deliver what is required. Show you can be counted on to get things done. When your network and connections know they can count on you to get the job done regardless of the situation, you become invaluable. For years, I had a picture at my desk that said, "Be a Yes in a Sea of No." I think that sums it up. Try to find a way to be a "Yes."

As you build your relationships and your ability to get things done within your organization, you are increasing your influence. Influence is critical. As you increase your influence, you increase your ability to be the kind of leader people want to follow and to have more opportunities presented to you that you want to pursue.

BUILD YOUR EXTERNAL NETWORK

As you build your career and your life, it's important to "constantly create the environment and community you want for yourself," says Keith Ferrazzi in the book *Never Eat Alone*. What are your interests? Who do you aspire to be? Who do you look up to? What job would you like to have in five, ten, or twenty years? When you dream about your future, what do you need to do to make it a reality? Once you have the answers to these questions, you can direct your activities accordingly.

Over the past twenty years, I have attended numerous conferences. You know the ones—very industry-specific where you earn continuing education credits to satisfy certain credentials and certifications. It was never about just the continuing education credits for me. While attending the conference, I was very intentional about ensuring I was connecting with other people. I attended the supplemental networking events. To connect, I reached out to conference coordinators and speakers. I asked how I could help them or get involved in their initiatives. I submitted proposals to be a speaker. As a result, I ended up getting selected for several committees and chosen to speak at multiple conferences. Making countless connections with people I continue to learn from today was invaluable. The process enabled me to learn and grow and have unique experiences that I would not have had otherwise.

Many years ago, I became interested in nonprofit board membership. I noticed that most senior leaders served on various boards of directors. Wanting to be a senior leader one day, I set out to learn more. I attended a board fair and learned about the missions of multiple organizations. I found one I believed in and was asked to join the board. Fast forward twenty years, and I have served as the president of that board and have been actively engaged over the years. It has enriched my life, taught me so much, and provided an opportunity for me to use my strengths and follow my interests.

I encourage you to get out there in the world and be an active participant, not just an observer. Talk to people. Get to know them. Learn from them. Determine how you can help them.

As Keith Ferrazzi has said, "Nothing in my life has created opportunity like a willingness to ask." You might be surprised how you can further your career by just asking for something. Ask for the job you want. Ask to join a group you are interested in. Ask to connect with someone you admire on LinkedIn. Ask how you might get involved in your community.

Not only will you become a more informed and interesting person through these opportunities, you will increase your personal connections and friendships. Research has shown that most people get jobs through personal connections. Other than my very first job, I don't think I've ever obtained a job that wasn't somehow due to my network and connections.

Take steps to maintain your connections and hopefully develop them into true friendships. Reach out to people for coffee, lunch, and cocktails. Send them thoughtful notes or small gifts. Recognize special days in their life. React to their posts on social media. The more time spent doing these things, the stronger your relationships will be.

• • • • •

Relationships are a critical part of success in both our professional and personal lives. Unicorn Leaders understand it's important to learn the techniques to get along with people and influence those around you. Take steps to increase your connections both within your organization and externally. Investing in relationships will ultimately enrich your career and your life. When you invest time and attention into cultivating relationships and lasting friendships, the rewards are magical.

UNICORN LEADER ACTION STEPS

- Take a quick fifteen-minute assessment on your current ability to lead up, across, and down at www.360DegreeLeader.com. You can gain insight to improve your leadership and develop the influence you need to achieve success!
- Write the names of five people that have been instrumental to your career or life success. How long has it been since you've talked to them? When was the last time you thanked them for their positive impact on your life? Reach out to them now and set up time for coffee, lunch, or just a phone call. Consider sending them a thoughtful note or card. Keeping your connections strong will strengthen your ability to achieve success and happiness.

CHAPTER ELEVEN

Evolve

By improving yourself, the world is made better. Be not afraid of growing too slowly. Be afraid only of standing still. Forget your mistakes but remember what they taught you.
—BENJAMIN FRANKLIN

The best leaders are always learning. We can't expect to achieve our full potential unless we take steps to evolve. To do this, we must proactively work on having a growth mindset, ensure we are taking steps to develop ourselves and our team, and get comfortable with change. To really excel and take ourselves to the highest level, it's critical to obtain the proper coaching. And as we move toward success, it's important to challenge ourselves to dream bigger. Let's look at some techniques to help ensure we are not standing still but forever moving forward and evolving to make our dreams come true.

GROWTH MINDSET

One of the keys to success depends upon your mindset. According to the research by Carol S. Dweck in the book *Mindset: The New Psychology of Success*, "People with a growth mindset believe that a person's true potential is unknown, while people with a fixed mindset believe you are born with certain qualities or abilities that determine your potential. A growth mindset is the belief that skills, intellect and talents can be developed through practice and perseverance. A fixed mindset is the belief that skills, intellect and talents are set and unchangeable."

Research has shown that a growth mindset drives motivation and, ultimately, achievement. Focusing on learning, growing, and improving can lead to greater success. Your true potential depends a lot on how hard you are willing to work and how much effort you put forth to reach your goals.

You can probably easily recognize people with a growth mindset. They tend to be the ones who embrace challenges, persist, and find inspiration in the success of others. They keep going when others want to quit. They realize that effort is required on the journey to success. They are lifelong learners.

Which do you think you have? As it turns out, we all have both mindsets. Therefore, we need to be proactive in strengthening our growth mindset. When you are focused on the belief that you can achieve greater success by learning more and putting in the effort to improve, you are using a growth mindset. Every day presents opportunities to grow and help those around you grow. This is a core tenet of Unicorn Leadership!

Obtaining a growth mindset is a journey—just like life . . . or becoming a Unicorn Leader.

However, it's not just your own mindset you need to be aware of. According to Carol S. Dweck, it's also important to be aware of the mindset of your boss and your organization as well. When bosses have a fixed mindset, they can force everyone into a fixed mindset. Fixed mindset leaders don't want great teams, because they need to be the smartest person in the room. When faced with this type of environment, growth-oriented employees freeze up. I've personally experienced this! At the time, I didn't realize that is why I felt so unconfident and afraid to suggest ideas, but that was exactly what was happening. I felt like the leaders around me were not interested in learning, and they definitely weren't interested in any feedback. I became focused on survival, and all creativity and motivation ceased to exist.

Just like it is important to align your values with your organization, it is also important to align your mindset. Otherwise, you might get a bad case of Sunday Sickness.

COACHING

"A coach is someone who tells you what you don't want to hear, who has you see what you don't want to see, so you can be who you have always known you could be," according to Tom Landry, the legendary coach of the Dallas Cowboys.

Are you coaching your team? The primary job of every leader is to help people grow, develop, and be successful in their job. Ensure you create an environment as a leader that provides your team members with tools and resources they need to do their job, as well as ongoing training and coaching to help them excel and grow. When a leader believes that people are the most important asset of an organization, they spend a lot of time thinking about how to help them be the very best they can be.

Are you getting the coaching you need? If you are fortunate enough to have an exceptional manager, you are likely getting frequent and ongoing feedback and coaching. Perhaps you have a regular one-to-one meeting with your manager in which your performance, objectives, development activities, recent successes, and any challenges are discussed. Hopefully, your manager gets to know your unique goals and aspirations. This is rare. I have known many leaders who don't see the importance of having regular meetings with their team members. And if they do meet, there is no coaching or focus on development. I have known leaders who never met with their direct reports unless there was some issue or urgent need. This is unacceptable. Remember, people need attention. And truly, if a leader is not focusing their efforts on helping their team members learn and grow and succeed, they are simply not a leader.

To really achieve exceptional performance, people need coaches. If you aren't getting the coaching and development from your manager, you must get it somewhere else. Consider mentors within your organization who are respected leaders. Consider hiring an executive coach or a life coach. It's vital that you take steps to discuss important aspects of your career with a trusted person so you can continue to improve and develop.

I've had a few executive coaches over the years, and each one has helped me become a better, stronger leader. Coaches can help you find the strength to get through challenging times, articulate your purpose and passion, update a resume or LinkedIn profile, or do new and scary things. A good coach will take time to understand you and your situation, as well as your goals, talents, and weaknesses. They will then provide you with tools, resources, guidance, and advice. What you do with this is up to you. You have to be coachable for it to work.

It's critical that you ask yourself: Am I coachable? According to the book *Trillion Dollar Coach* by Eric Schmidt, Jonathan Rosenberg, and Alan Eagle, the traits that make a person coachable include honesty and humility, the willingness to persevere and work hard, and a constant openness to learning. Do you open yourself up to accept things that may be hard to hear, listen without prejudice, and then commit to taking steps to improve? You have to do all of this for coaching to pay off. But it is so worth it!

I recently had a coach tell me I was not producing the best work I could because I wasn't stopping when I got tired. I was getting tired, then lazy, then messy, and then not producing my best work. She told me I need to take a break. Step away. She made me write it down: Step Away. My immediate thought was, *I have to keep going. I'll never meet my (self-imposed) deadline. I'll never get done what I need to get done.* My next thought was, *Listen to her and step away.* So, I did. I took the break she told me to take and came back to what I was doing more refreshed and energized. And I produced better results!

Remember, the world's best athletes need coaches, so why wouldn't you? Coaches can observe you in action and help you get better if you will listen and learn.

DEVELOP AND GROW

Becoming a good leader is a lifelong learning process. If you want to succeed in a career or in life, you need to learn as much as you can. Author and leadership expert John Maxwell says two of the most important questions to ask are:

- What am I doing to develop myself?
- What am I doing to develop my staff?

A Unicorn Leader must constantly ask these questions . . . and make sure the answer is never "Nothing!"

Be proactive in your own development and growth. Not sure where to start? Here are a few suggestions:

- Read books on how to become a better leader (see the References, Recommended Reading, and Resources section later in this book as a starting point)
- Read industry articles, subscribe to podcasts, and watch relevant YouTube videos
- Attend training, conferences, and webinars
- Consider obtaining professional certifications in areas of interest
- Take an online course you find interesting (Coursera has some great options!)

When you do these proactive learning activities, you learn more not only about a certain topic but also about yourself. You will stumble onto ideas or innovative solutions that you may never have seen or explored before. From these activities, you will learn more about who you want to become and what you aspire to be.

Be curious! Never stop learning, and you will never stop growing. This ongoing curiosity will take you to interesting places on your journey and will expand your life in ways you never dreamed.

Then, be a multiplier and share what you learn with your team members. Help expand the education of your team in staff meetings and one-to-one meetings. Provide them with summaries of a training you attended or facilitate a discussion on a recent course you took. Taking these steps will help ensure the strength of your team and the overall success of your organization.

CHANGE

I love the quote "If nothing changes, nothing changes." I had this written on a whiteboard for several years to remind me every day of the importance of change. Change is hard. Change can be shocking, scary, and exciting. It can cause us to experience grief, loss, confusion, hope, and joy. Change is complex. It causes us to feel so many different emotions—sometimes all at once and sometimes over a longer time frame. I have always believed that to be a great leader, you must be a change agent. You must constantly work to become comfortable with change. Change is a part of life, part of a career, part of raising kids, part of marriage, part of our existence. Take steps to embrace it instead of resisting it, and you will be happier and more successful.

I have shown my teams the Kubler-Ross Change Curve a hundred times over the years. (I encourage you to find it on Google and see what you think.) This change curve is a very effective way to illustrate all the emotions we go through in the change process. When a change is announced, we may experience various feelings initially, such as shock, mourning, turmoil, rage, and feelings of loss. As time goes on and we process the change, our feelings become more positive as we accept and adapt to the situation.

It is a great reminder that it's okay—we ALL feel this way. We are ALL going through multiple emotions during a change process, but we will get through it together, and we will be stronger than we were before.

Change events challenge us to grow. Change events provide opportunities to learn new things, do things a different way, expand our way of thinking, try things we never thought of, and evolve. But, again, change is hard. That's why there so many books written about it from *Who Moved My Cheese?* to *Our Iceberg Is Melting*. There is an industry devoted to change management and certifications to obtain on this topic. If change were an easy undertaking, there would not be so much material written on how to do it, get through it, survive it, and thrive in it.

Sometimes, it's not just about how we react to changes that are occurring around us; it's about how we take steps to change—or evolve—so we can become better leaders. In the book by Marshall Goldsmith, *What Got You Here Won't Get You There,* he encourages us not to be delusional about our success, to learn from our behavior, and to course correct when needed so we can be better and do better.

As an executive coach, Marshall Goldsmith requires a 360-degree feedback survey for his clients as a starting point for coaching. Have you participated in a 360-degree feedback survey? I was fortunate to get to do this many years ago. This is when your boss, your direct reports, and your peers complete a survey about you. It is extremely enlightening and helps you realize that everyone sees you a bit differently. It also helps you understand what you are doing well and what you need to improve. I believe it would be worthwhile for any organization to offer this as part of any people leader development program. I truly don't think a person can reach their potential without an all-encompassing understanding of how their actions and behaviors affect everyone around them.

Once you have results from a survey like this, you can improve only if you accept the feedback and commit to change what needs to be changed.

Many people have the deluded idea that they have been successful so far, so they must be doing things right. Why change what is clearly working? But we must! We have to keep growing and learning and evolving if we want to be successful in the future. The world is changing. Nothing is static, so why would you choose to be?

I love the 20 Bad Habits that Marshall Goldsmith says we need to watch out for and correct if we want to better ensure future success. The Bad Habits list forces us to evaluate our own personal habits and determine things such as:

- Do I need to add my two cents to every discussion?
- Do I constantly use sarcasm as an approach to be witty?
- Do I impose my standards on others?
- Do I tend to blame everyone but myself?

I encourage you to review the 20 Bad Habits for yourself and assess whether they might possibly be impacting your performance and potential. I know I have some of these habits, and I know I need to work hard to make sure they don't hold me back. Now that I'm aware, I am more likely to catch myself—and stop myself—from adding my two cents to every discussion. I try really hard to not impose my standards on others. It's still hard, but once you are aware and have a true desire to get better, you can take steps to change. Which of these do you need to work on?

DREAM BIGGER

When you focus on growth and learning, you might surprise yourself with what you accomplish. This will likely cause you to realize you need to dream bigger. We tend to set the bar low sometimes for certain goals or dreams for various reasons—maybe we lack confidence, maybe we don't want to be disappointed, or maybe we are scared. I encourage you to take steps to raise the bar and loosen your self-imposed limits on what you think you can achieve.

One way to go about this is to stop avoiding things that scare you. Speaking at a conference or presenting at an important meeting? Attending an industry group event and participating on a panel? Participating on a committee or special initiative? Posting a thought leadership article on LinkedIn? Think of some activities that interest you but scare you. Consider some events you would love to be a part of but the thought makes you nervous. Envision something that would be really cool to do but also very challenging and gives you butterflies just thinking about it.

These are exactly the things you should be pursuing! I encourage you to take steps to seek out these opportunities and pay attention when these opportunities drop into your lap. Don't make excuses to yourself or others about why you "aren't available" or are "too busy." You need to make yourself available to grow, develop, and do scary things. Trust me, no one finds great success by sitting at home watching a Netflix series. You have to get out there in the world and participate in interesting things that are a little scary sometimes.

In the book *Year of Yes*, Shonda Rhimes sums it up:

"Yes to everything scary. Yes to everything that takes me out of my comfort zone. Yes to everything that feels like it might be crazy. Yes to everything that feels out of character. Yes to everything that feels goofy. Yes to everything. Everything. Say yes. Saying yes is courage. Saying yes is the sun. Saying yes is life."

Yes! One hundred percent Yes!

As Eleanor Roosevelt said, "You must do the thing you think you cannot do." My all-time favorite song is "Dream On" by Steven Tyler. I love it so much that my family has instructions to play it at my funeral. I'm serious about the power of having dreams and trying to make them come true. I keep a reminder at my desk that says, "If your dreams don't scare you, dream bigger." I want to be constantly reminded to not get too comfortable in my comfort zone, to not set the bar too low, and to always dream bigger.

One technique to keep us focused on bigger dreams is to create a vision board. A vision board is a place to compile your hopes, dreams, and aspirations. It can be in any format that works for you and contain anything that provides you with inspiration. My vision board is a twelve-inch-by-twelve-inch corkboard and has a variety of things on it, such as my values, inspirational quotes, pictures of places I want to travel, a faux picture of me on the cover of Forbes magazine, and a unicorn. Occasionally, I add things or revise what's on it. It's just a fun way to keep those dreams front and center. Because it's in a location I see several times a day, it keeps me mindful to keep dreaming and keep working on those dreams.

Do you have a vision board? I encourage you to try it out. I do believe when we think about what we want, write it down, and focus on it, magical things can happen, and we can begin to manifest our dreams. Give it a try! Allow yourself to unleash a bit of creativity into the universe and see where it might lead.

It's critical to evolve. There are actionable steps we can take to become the best leader we can. We must continue to learn and develop ourselves and our team. Keeping our minds open and our dreams front and center will create new opportunities as we continue our journey to become a Unicorn Leader.

UNICORN LEADER ACTION STEPS

- Do you have a growth mindset? Take the mindset assessment at blog.mindsetworks.com/what-s-my-mindset and explore resources and tools to help develop your growth mindset.
- Review Marshall Goldsmith's The 20 Bad Habits article from the book *What Got You Here Won't Get You There.* Take steps to break any bad habits you currently struggle with.
- Remind yourself "If your dreams don't scare you, dream bigger" and create your personal vision board that illustrates your biggest dreams.
- Consider getting guidance from a mentor, executive coach, or life coach to help you become the best leader and person you can be.

CHAPTER TWELVE

Self-Compassion

A moment of self-compassion can change your entire day. A string of such moments can change the course of your life. —CHRISTOPHER K. GERMER

It is important to be kind to ourselves. It may seem like that goes against our efforts to become stronger and more successful, but it actually can enhance these areas. Focusing on self-care, considering counseling when needed, and embracing overall well-being can be a big improvement in your life. Learning how to be happier with ourselves and our life is a gift. With awareness and intentional actions, we can live a more fulfilling life. Let's explore more about this and start living our best life!

SELF-CARE

Sadly, I used to think self-compassion and self-care was a bunch of nonsense. I was raised to be "tough," got through multiple challenges in my life by being "tough," and just kept trying to get "tougher." My cousin has always told me, "Be kind to yourself," and I wouldn't or couldn't listen to that advice. Especially since I became a working mom, it was *Go! Go! Go!* Even though I would get multiple reminders from people to "put on my oxygen mask first," I didn't.

That said, I did exercise, I usually got enough sleep, and I did get a massage on a regular basis. So there was some self-care going on. But what was missing was down time. Quiet time. Time to think. Silence. And then, 2020 showed up and brought along a year of no travel, no activities, canceled plans, and a stay-at-home approach. It turned out to be one of the best years of my life. I was able to learn to take better care of myself, let go of some harsh self-criticism, and put some real focus on being kind to myself.

In the book *Good to Great*, Jim Collins wrote: "Most of us lead busy, but undisciplined lives. We have ever-expanding to-do lists, trying to build momentum by doing, doing, doing—and doing more. And it rarely works. Those who build the good-to-great companies, however, made as much use of stop-doing lists as the to-do lists."

This is true not only for companies but for individuals. I've come to learn the importance of stop doing and know it is key to growth and happiness. Putting some thought into what you might stop doing will help you set better expectations and boundaries for yourself and for your self-care.

Self-care is about awareness. Being aware of how you are treating yourself is the first step to treating yourself better.

Have you paid attention to your self-talk? I had not. But when I started to, I heard, *Why are you so dumb? Why did you say that? How could you not have known that? You are so stupid! You will never be good enough to do that. Your facial expressions are so idiotic! Your presentation is going to be terrible. You're terrible. Why aren't you more ______________________ (articulate, intelligent, pulled together, etc.)?* Would you say those things to a friend? No! So stop saying them to yourself.

Many years ago, in Kentucky, I was working on a project. One morning, during the first few days the project was kicking off, I was on the elevator with several people. One of the newly hired people said to themselves (but out loud for everyone to hear): "I don't know whoever thought I was smart enough to do this job." That comment has stuck with me for twenty years! We ALL have thought that. We think things like that almost every day, although most of us stop ourselves from saying it out loud. We need to take it a step further and STOP saying it at all. We are not being kind to ourselves.

I have found the Center for Mindful Self-Compassion to be such a helpful resource for improving my focus on self-care and compassion. It starts with this definition of self-compassion:

Self-compassion is really no different than having compassion for others. You feel warmth, caring, and a desire to help the suffering person in some way. Having compassion means that you offer understanding and kindness to others when they fail or make mistakes, rather than judging them harshly. It involves acting the same way toward yourself when you are having a difficult time, fail, or notice something you don't like about yourself.

Instead of ignoring your pain and mercilessly judging and criticizing yourself for various inadequacies or shortcomings, self-compassion means you are kind and understanding when confronted with personal failings. There are many exercises you can do to help you improve your self-compassion, including meditation and journaling. But one of the easiest exercises is to just ask yourself: How would you treat a friend? Try responding to yourself in the same way you would respond to a close friend when they are suffering. Give yourself a break. You are not perfect; none of us are. Show yourself some grace and understanding.

As Dr. Kristen Neff explains at www.selfcompassion.org: "Self-compassion is a practice of goodwill, not good feelings. In other words, even though the friendly, supportive stance of self-compassion is aimed at the alleviation of suffering, we can't always control the way things are. If we use self-compassion practice to try to make our pain go away by suppressing it or fighting against it, things will likely just get worse. With self-compassion we mindfully accept that the moment is painful, and embrace ourselves with kindness and care in response, remembering that imperfection is part of the shared human experience. This allows us to hold ourselves in love and connection, giving ourselves the support and comfort needed to bear the pain, while providing the optimal conditions for growth and transformation."

"Remembering that imperfection is part of the shared human experience" is critical. I have come to realize that I am so hard on myself because I'm expecting perfectionism from myself. One of my core values is excellence, but I had morphed that into "perfection." No one is perfect and nothing is perfect. I have to train myself to let go of unrealistic expectations each and every day.

In her book *I Thought it Was Just Me (But It Isn't)*, Brene Brown encourages us to learn to respond to ourselves with empathy and understanding. We all need to guard against harsh self-judgment and feelings of shame. We must be cautious to not enforce expectations of ourselves that we get from the media, society, or other sources. She provides some reality check questions:

- How realistic are these expectations?
- Can I be all these things all of the time? Do I want to be?
- Can all of these characteristics exist in one authentic person?

When we experience shame, we have intense feelings of believing we are flawed or unworthy; the opposite of experiencing shame is experiencing empathy.

I love the quote from Anna Quindlen: "The thing that is really hard, and really amazing, is giving up on being perfect and beginning the work of becoming yourself."

COUNSELING

At one point in my career, I realized there was something more I needed than an executive coach. I needed professional counseling. My feelings of failure, low self-worth, and overall frustration were overwhelming. I was running, being coached, and taking steps to "be better," but it didn't seem to be enough. So I found a licensed therapist and made time for the sessions. My counselor talked to me about self-compassion and perfectionism. She gave me exercises to think through things and work through my emotions—everything from deep breathing, to sitting in silence and just listening, to writing things down and journaling.

Part of self-compassion is getting yourself the help you need. If you haven't tried counseling, I would encourage you to give it a try. So often, we are dealing with bigger root-cause issues and, through counseling, we can find ways to deal with those issues and even move past them. Get the help you need so you can live the best life you can!

WELL-BEING

In 2020, I found the course The Science of Well-Being was available on Coursera, and I decided to take it. It was a great experience, and I gained a lot of valuable insight. I also read the book *The Happiness Advantage* by Shawn Achor, which aligned with—and supplemented—the course teachings. Since happiness is one of my core values, I am very interested in this topic.

Ask yourself now, on a scale of 1-5, "How happy am I?"

Answer: ____________________

Most of us think that things and accomplishments make us happy. A new car. A bigger house. Getting a promotion. Making more money. As it turns out, the research shows these things don't bring us long-term happiness. Happiness is actually an ***intentional journey*** that we can take! By focusing on the areas below, we can increase our happiness.

Gratitude is a positive emotional state in which one recognizes and appreciates what one has received in life. Research shows that taking time to experience gratitude can make you happier and even healthier. Each day, take time to write down a few things for which you are grateful. Also, think of someone who has made a positive impact on your life. Write them a letter to thank them for how they have touched your life and tell them why they are such a meaningful part of your life.

I started a gratitude journal at the beginning of the year to intentionally incorporate this aspect into my daily life. What are you grateful for?

Savoring is the act of stepping outside of an experience to review and appreciate it. Savoring intensifies and lengthens the positive emotions that come with doing something you love. Each day, take time to savor an experience—a hot shower, a nice meal, a beautiful day outside. Enjoy these moments and let them soak in. Think about how lucky you are to enjoy such an amazing moment in life.

Do you let yourself really enjoy that hot shower in the morning? What about that nice birthday meal? I feel that savoring and gratitude are very closely connected. When I am intentional about savoring, I immediately am overwhelmed with gratitude.

Random acts of kindness can improve our lives. Research shows that happy people are motivated to do kind things for others. Try to do something kind each day, such as write a thank-you note, contribute to a cause you believe in, or buy the person's coffee behind you at Starbucks. Doing things that help or positively impact others does wonders for the soul.

When is the last time you did something totally unexpected and thoughtful for someone?

Social connection drives happiness. When we take time to genuinely connect with others, we can boost our mood. Research shows that happy people spend more time with others. Take some time each day to connect with others and spend time talking with people. Reach out and ask a friend about their day or catch up with a family member.

When is the last time you really connected with someone? Not just brief texting but really got caught up on someone's life, struggles, and current state of happiness?

Sleep is critical for optimal well-being. One of the reasons we are so unhappy in life is due to our lack of sleep. Try to get at least seven hours of sleep every night. Sleep will make you feel better and will improve your mood.

How much sleep do you get consistently? I feel so much better and am more productive when I get a good eight hours!

Exercise can boost your mood and help make you healthier overall. Research suggests just thirty minutes a day will help you feel much better.

Exercise is the most underused "drug" for depression, but it really can help you feel better in so many areas of your life.

Meditation is a practice of turning your attention away from distracting thoughts toward a single point of reference (breathing, compassion, specific topic). Research shows that meditation can improve your mood and increase concentration. Spend just ten minutes a day meditating, and you will likely see the benefit.

Have you tried the Kirtan Kriya meditation of *Sa Ta Na Ma*? Google it and give it a try! I have tried to do this more over the past year, and I find it very valuable. Sa = birth and beginning, Ta = life and existence, Na = death and change, and Ma = rebirth and regeneration.

Meditation has helped provide improved clarity about my goals and is useful to just clear my mind. It has helped me articulate what exactly it is that I want from each day, each week, and my life in general. I have found great meditation options on Netflix, SoundCloud, YouTube, and multiple other free resources.

I encourage you to take intentional steps to increase the happiness in your life. Try some of these activities each day for a month and then ask yourself again: *How happy am I?* I'm predicting a positive change in your score and in your overall sense of well-being.

Take as much time to care for yourself as you do others. Give yourself a break. Treat yourself with kindness and compassion. Unicorn Leaders understand that the journey is long and can be very exhausting, and they must occasionally rest and recover in order to properly manifest the universe. Use some of the resources here to be more mindful about how you can improve your self-care. Seek out assistance when needed to help you on your journey of healing and self-compassion. Take intentional steps to be happier in your life by focusing on the activities that truly lead to happiness. When you do these things, it will allow you to continue on your journey of becoming all you can be and be further prepared to reach your highest potential.

UNICORN LEADER ACTION STEPS

- Try the guided meditation or self-compassion exercises at www.selfcompassion.org.
- Watch the Netflix series *Headspace: Guide to Meditation*.
- Take thirty minutes for yourself to exercise, meditate, write in a journal, or express gratitude.

CHAPTER THIRTEEN

Authentic Leadership

When you are your authentic self, people will respond.
—ROBIN ROBERTS

Imagine if you embraced your authentic self and encouraged others to do the same. Imagine if, each day, authenticity and inclusion were integrated into our lives. Imagine how empowered we would all be as employees, leaders, and human beings. We could more easily follow our dreams and live our life to the fullest. By examining the concepts of authenticity and inclusion, we can figure out how to do just that.

AUTHENTICITY

I completed an amazing virtual workshop, The Badass Workshop 1 and 2, curated by Bozoma Saint John—the CMO of Netflix. It was one of the most impactful learning experiences I've had. I found her to be very inspirational and very authentic. She definitely encourages authenticity. She told us to "Lead the chorus. If your audience doesn't like what you are singing—find another audience." And "Focus on who you are and what you bring and show up in full celebration of who you are."

It can be challenging to be your authentic self. Sometimes it's hard because we are afraid others won't accept us for how we are, so we adjust our personality or "tone it down." Other times, it's hard because we haven't fully embraced or accepted ourselves as good enough, smart enough, pretty enough, or just ENOUGH.

As Luvvie Ajayi Jones says in her book *Professional Troublemaker*: "When we talk about people being their full selves and how a lot of people are afraid of it, it's not that people don't want to show up as themselves. It's that they know that when they show up in their full splendor, they will be judged for it. Being ordinary and unremarkable is hardly a life goal, but we are often scared into being that way."

As an individual, the sooner in life you can figure out who you truly are and how you are wired, the better. And the sooner you can ACCEPT who you truly are, EMBRACE it, and CELEBRATE it, the sooner you will be on the path to increased happiness and success. All of that is much easier said than done.

When I had my first child, I quit my job and decided to be a stay-at-home mom. That's what my mom did when I was a baby, that's what many of my friends and family members did, and so that's what I did. I made it five months before I called my previous employer and asked to come back in any capacity.

I felt like a terrible mother and a terrible person. But I wasn't happy. I felt like I wasn't "me." So I went back to work. My mother had a fit! She tried to convince me that I "didn't need to work" and I needed to stay home. I felt guilty, and I didn't need more guilt. I tried to explain how I felt to her and what I needed, but she couldn't understand. And I know many others can't understand. But my "blueprint" needs to work. Having a career is imprinted in my soul. I chose to embrace myself and my need to work. I was true to myself, and I have never had any regrets about going back to work or being a working mom. Never.

In the book *Untamed*, Glennon Doyle sums it up brilliantly: "Every time you're given a choice between disappointing someone else and disappointing yourself, your duty is to disappoint that someone else. Your job, throughout your entire life, is to disappoint as many people as it takes to avoid disappointing yourself." Yes!

For most, finding your authentic self is a journey that can take decades or almost a lifetime. If you haven't yet begun this journey, I encourage you to start today. I think the best place to start is to determine your values and strengths and then examine your core personality traits. I encourage you to really examine what you have loved about certain jobs and hated about others. Spend some time in silence and meditation. Ask yourself what you would regret most if you found out you had six months to live. Pay attention to what brings you joy. Learn to listen to yourself—to your soul—and learn to let that voice guide you in your journey.

Encouraging people to bring their whole self or authentic self to work is something too few leaders or organizations do. I believe the best leaders are accepting of the uniqueness we all bring to the universe. They realize that by allowing our authentic self to show up, they are also allowing our creativity, fresh ideas, and out-of-the-box thinking to show up—and we need more of that!

The best leaders are themselves. And the best leaders want their employees to be themselves. It is really that simple.

Think about the best boss/mentor/leader that you ever had. What characteristics and qualities come to mind? *Inspiring. Visionary. Trusted. Encouraging. Fun.* These are some of the words I think of when I think about that person. But also, I am reminded that they provided a sense of belonging and allowed me to be myself.

INCLUSION

Why is it so hard to be authentic? I suppose one reason is we are scared we won't be accepted or included if we are our true selves. To really thrive in your career and in your life, it is critical to work somewhere that has a culture of inclusion and focuses on providing progressive stages of inclusion.

As Frances Frei and Anne Morriss share in the book *Unleashed*, a culture of inclusion in the workplace makes employees feel "safe, welcome, celebrated, and cherished."

How would you rate your current workplace? How would you rate yourself as a leader in providing these levels of inclusion?

When you find yourself working somewhere that has an inclusive culture, it is so freeing and empowering. You feel like you can accomplish anything because everyone is bringing their whole self and their best self along with their ideas, energies, and positive vibes. It's magical!

On the other hand, when you find yourself working somewhere that doesn't welcome you, doesn't reward your unique ideas, and doesn't view individual uniqueness as a competitive advantage, you feel that as well. You feel like your soul is being crushed, you aren't worthy, and there is something wrong with you. It's important to remove yourself from that type of environment as soon as you possibly can.

Authentic leadership is about making your team feel safe. It's about sacrificing for your people. Here's a way to measure authenticity in a leader: Do they take a pay cut when pay cuts are implemented across the organization? Do they give themselves a bonus when no one else gets a bonus?

Once, I was given a bonus but one of my team members was not given one. This team member had worked so hard in the previous year. The only reason the division had accomplished its goals was because of her efforts. I asked why she wasn't getting a bonus and was told the head of the organization didn't feel she deserved one. My response was she deserved one more than I did and my bonus should be given to her. This response shocked my boss and the head of the organization so much that they ended up giving her a bonus—and letting me keep mine. It was a nice ending to the situation, but I was completely serious and would have happily given her my bonus.

When you are an authentic leader, you look out for people. You take care of them, and you sacrifice for them.

At some point in my career, I became aware that certain people have employment contracts. Those at the highest levels and with the most perceived value had contracts. When a change occurred at the top or when they were let go, they didn't have to worry because they received at least a year's salary, benefits, and other perks. As I started to pay closer attention, I began to realize those individuals were held prisoner by employment contracts and it impacted their authenticity. They were more willing to "go along to get along," and no matter what they were told from the top, they shut their mouth and just did it. They seemed to be held hostage by these contracts. They seemed less willing to advocate for their employees in some cases and could no longer be the sole owner of their destiny. Be aware of situations that impact your authenticity and the course of your destiny.

• • • • •

A Unicorn Leader is an authentic leader. Take some time to consider your authentic self and how you are wired. Are you bringing your whole self to work and to life? Are you encouraging authenticity and inclusion? Take steps to make your team feel safe and celebrated. Take care of your team and look out for them. Listen to your soul. Remember not to disappoint yourself. Instead, be true to you and open yourself up to an extraordinary life that comes about by embracing your unique self.

UNICORN LEADER ACTION STEPS

- Sign up for The Badass Workshop curated by Bozoma Saint John.
- Watch Simon Sinek's TED Talk on why good leaders make you feel safe: www.ted.com/talks/simon_sinek_why_good_leaders_make_you_feel_safe.

CHAPTER FOURTEEN

Courage

You must do the things you think you cannot do.
—ELEANOR ROOSEVELT

To live life as we are meant to live takes courage. To get the job we want takes courage. To achieve our dreams takes courage. Life is not perfect, and the days can be hard. To get up, keep working, and try again—this all takes courage. It requires us to focus on doing things with more audacity and daring. Being intentional about our wishes and coming up with a plan to overcome the obstacles in our way is a requirement to reach our destiny.

DOING

When we are in touch with our authentic self and we have an understanding of how we are wired and what type of things fulfill us, this is KNOWING. Next, we have to get on with the business of DOING. We must take action. We must take the steps to get us moving along on the journey of our life and all that we are meant to do. In the book *Untamed*, Glennon Doyle encourages us to "shorten the gap between the Knowing and the Doing." But fear creeps in, and we start to question the Doing. As she says in her book: "We say,

'Maybe it's safer to just stay here. Even if it's not true enough, maybe it's good enough.' But good enough is what makes people drink too much and snark too much and become bitter and sick and live in quiet desperation until they lie on their deathbed and wonder—what kind of life/relationship/family/world might I have created if I'd been braver?"

Diane Ackerman, author and poet, said, "I don't want to get to the end of my life and find I just lived the length of it . . . I want to live the width of it as well."

If we aren't careful, we will wake up and wonder how our life passed us by and we didn't do any of the things we wanted to. Do you have dreams of writing a book? Getting a degree or certification? Speaking at a conference? Hosting a podcast? Launching a business? If you aren't taking intentional steps each day to accomplish these things, you are taking intentional steps toward regret.

Gary Vaynerchuk, chairman of VaynerX, shares his inspiration very simply: *You're going to die. Do something about it!*

Exactly! So I say, let's not just dream about our dreams—let's take action to achieve them!

Why are we so afraid to do the things we dream about? Perhaps we think we can't afford it, shouldn't risk it, or would likely fail. Maybe we are concerned what our mother/sister/father/daughter/friend would think. Possibly we think we will start tomorrow/next week/next year/when the time is right. What if we just decided to go for it since we only have one life to live? Let's find the courage to contribute our talents, strengths, and uniqueness to the universe and stop wasting precious time.

We must stop NOT doing things because we are afraid. Take the first step. Then the next step. The goal you are pursuing can be reached one step—and one deep breath—at a time.

AUDACITY

Luvvie Ajayi Jones, author and speaker, reminds us that "The lives we live are full of people's dreams realized. The things we use every day are born from the audacity of someone who thought it was possible." Yes!

Are you familiar with "BHAGs" (bee-hags)? BHAGs are Big Hairy Audacious Goals. This concept was introduced in the book *Built to Last* written by James Collins and Jerry Porras. The research indicated that "Highly visionary companies often use BHAGs to stimulate progress. A BHAG is clear and compelling and serves as a focal point of effort. It engages people because it is tangible, energizing and highly focused. People get it right away and it creates team spirit. It helps fight against complacency. To set a BHAG, an organization must have an enormous amount of self-confidence and commitment; and the BHAG should fall outside the comfort zone."

While this concept in *Built to Last* was discussed in terms of business goals and organizational strategy, I submit that it can be a strategy for individuals to apply to their lives. We all have goals, but we need to raise the bar on our goals and make them a bit bigger, a whole lot hairier, and more audacious. Make sure you haven't become too complacent in your own life. Are you just going through the motions or are you forcing yourself to STRETCH and grow? Are you doing things that are comfortable or things that take courage?

One of my BHAGs in life is to write a book. Here I am writing a book! This is definitely a BHAG—it's clear and has a focal point of effort. It requires me to be highly focused, and the end goal (the book) is tangible. Working on something you believe in is very energizing. I absolutely have to work on my self-confidence and commitment every day—and I am way outside my comfort zone. I have no idea what I'm doing! But it has always been a goal, so I found a way to figure it out, make progress, and fulfill my dream. (If you are reading this now, I achieved a BHAG!)

You can do it too. Think about your goals. Now, magnify them—make them big, hairy, and audacious!

DARING

A few years back, I was working on an incredibly challenging, dysfunctional, and extremely political project and was feeling very frustrated and lost. I was leading an effort that had been discussed as necessary for years, but no one had committed to doing it until then. Knowing it was the right thing for the organization, I had believed in it for years. But I felt like I was getting kicked in the teeth and stabbed in the back every single day.

I came across this quote from Theodore Roosevelt: "It is not the critic who counts; not the man who points out how the strong man stumbles, or where the doer of deeds could have done them better. The credit belongs to the man who is actually in the arena, whose face is marred by dust and sweat and blood; who strives valiantly; who errs, who comes short again and again, because there is no effort without error and shortcoming; but who does actually strive to do the deeds; who knows great enthusiasms, the great devotions; who spends himself in a worthy cause; who at the best knows in the end the triumph of high achievement, and who at the worst, if he fails, at least fails while daring greatly."

This brought me a lot of peace. It was me—and my team—whose face was marred by dust and sweat and blood. It was the critics who were kicking us in the teeth and stabbing us in the back—but they were conveniently NOT in the arena. I realized that whatever happened, my team and I had great enthusiasm and devotion. If we failed, we would do it while daring greatly. And, suddenly, that was enough. At least I had the courage to pursue something I knew was right, and I attempted hard things. Success or failure, I dared greatly. I had courage. What do you need the courage to do?

Brent Gleeson, author of *Embrace the Suck*, reminds us, "When the hell have you ever accomplished anything spectacular while nestled safely in your comfort zone? We both know the answer. Never." He goes on to say, "Once you have clearly defined goals, you know what stands in your way. The question is, how bad do you want to conquer those goals? How willing are you to embrace the suck?"

Think of all the goals you've had over the course of your life. I'm sure there were some you accomplished and some you did not. In either case—you survived, you learned, you grew, you tried. Now, think of all the goals you still have. What is currently standing in your way of achieving them? Figure out a way to overcome the obstacles and reach your goals.

WOOP

The "WOOP" method was developed by Dr. Gabriele Oettingen. WOOP combines mental contrasting and implementation intentions that have been proven to help people adjust behavior and achieve their goals.

Being able to articulate your Wish, the Outcome you are hoping for, the Obstacles that stand in your way, and the Plan to actually achieve your goals will help move you along in your journey. The WOOP method (Wish, Outcome, Obstacle, Plan) helps you pave the way to making your dreams a reality. One of the best things about it is that it forces you to form a contingency plan and prepare for your obstacles. It is based on years of scientific research, and I can attest that it works! There is even an app you can download to assist you with this technique.

Let's try it now:

- What is a goal you have? A dream or a wish?
- What is the outcome of accomplishing that goal or wish? How will you feel when you achieve it?
- What are some obstacles that may get in your way? What distractions or temptations will you encounter?

- How will you deal with those obstacles? What will you do to overcome the distractions and remain focused on achieving your dream?

By visualizing this and crafting a plan now to deal with obstacles later, you are increasing your odds of success because you have a strategy. This technique has been shown to effectively modify habits and provide a straightforward way to achieving your goals. Give it a try! What do you have to lose? It's an intentional action you can take to get one step closer to seeing your wishes come true. Tony Robbins, motivational speaker and author, says, "The path to success is to take massive, determined actions."

I encourage you to start taking determined actions today!

DESTINY

In the book *The War of Art,* Steven Pressfield writes: "Most of us have two lives. The life we live, and the unlived life within us. Between the two stands Resistance . . . Resistance will tell you anything to keep you from doing your work. Resistance is always lying and always full of shit . . . This very moment, we can change our lives. There never was a moment, and never will be, when we are without the power to alter our destiny. This second, we can turn the tables on Resistance. This second, we can sit down and do our work . . . What finally convinced me to go ahead was simply that I was so unhappy not going ahead."

He goes on to say: "The more scared we are of a work or calling, the more sure we can be that we have to do it."

I first read those words at a time when I was very unhappy in a job and my inner voice was whispering BHAGs on a daily basis. It was like being struck by lightning. Those words were for me and my fight against resistance. They helped inspire me to stop being complacent and unhappy and instead be accepting of fear and take the steps to alter my destiny. We cannot be afraid of fear and live the life we are meant to live. Embrace the fear! How terrible to get to the end of your life and be asked what, if anything, held you back from doing all you had dreamed—and your answer was fear.

As William Irvine, author of *The Stoic Challenge*, says, "When we examine the lives of accomplished individuals, we find almost without exception that they pursued goals that were difficult to attain, experienced many failures trying to attain them, and nevertheless pressed on. There is something much worse than failing to do something difficult, and that is not even attempting to do it because you feared failure."

At some point, we may find ourselves in a job or relationship that is driving us crazy. We think, *Surely this cannot be my destiny.* Take some time to assess any situation you are in and determine your options. Don't be reactive but take intentional steps to take control of your destiny.

Dr. Mike Bechtle, bestselling author of five books, encourages us to use a three-step process:

1. First, try to change the situation using logic and influence to adjust the dynamics of the situation.
2. Get advice from mentors or colleagues who have been in a similar situation.
3. Next, work on your attitude. Be intentional about being the victor, not the victim of any situation. Take determined actions to learn from the situation.

Additionally, assess if the situation is worth staying in and continuing to work through. Make sure you have invested the time in a carefully thought-out process to decide what you need in order to ensure your health, happiness and overall well-being.

Take some time to sit in silence, meditate, and listen. Listen to your soul. Block out the other voices. The voices of resistance, the friend who mocks your BHAG, the doubt of your mother. Block out all the voices except your authentic, true self—and listen to that voice. Listen to your soul to manifest your destiny.

• • • • •

Whether it's a bad job situation or you need to take steps to fight complacency and do the things you've always wanted to do—have courage. A Unicorn Leader will embrace the fear. Come up with a plan and a strategy to get you on your way toward greatness and happiness. Don't let the coziness of comfort continue to trap you in mediocrity. As Brent Gleeson says, "We cloak ourselves in mediocrity when we are unwilling to embrace the challenges that stand in our way of greatness." Remove that cloak and move with determination and courage toward your dreams.

UNICORN LEADER ACTION STEP

- Use WOOP to find and fulfill your wishes: woopmylife.org/en/home.

Conclusion

While I've dreamed about and talked about writing a book for years, it was really put into motion on a beautiful September day in 2020. I was enjoying a weekend trip with some of my best friends. On our last day, as we were gathering up and preparing to head to the airport, I went outside to have just one more moment to take in the beautiful surroundings. I wanted to think about my gratitude for the trip, my friends, and my life. Sitting down in a chair, I embraced the beauty and the silence. What happened next is something I can't really explain. I've never experienced it before in my life. I didn't hear a voice or see a vision. But I felt to the depth of my soul that I needed to quit my job and write a book. I felt an overwhelming force that convinced me I needed to give myself a chance to do other things. And so . . . I did!

When I arrived home from that trip, I told my husband I planned to quit my job and write a book. Thankfully, he was supportive and agreed to help me craft a plan. We took steps to ensure finances were in order. I made time for meditation and reflection to ensure my mindset was where it needed to be for this to be successful. Taking time to really think about what I wanted out of life and what regrets I would have if I didn't allow myself the opportunity to take a chance on myself was invaluable. I came up with a realistic timeline and plan of action. And then, events unfolded that confirmed this plan was valid and needed to happen. The universe was talking to me, and I chose to listen.

Thank you for joining me on this part of my journey. I hope what I've learned and the experiences I've shared in this book have been of some value to you. I encourage you to Map Your (Unicorn Leader) Journey in the following section so you can better understand yourself and where you want to go. I challenge you to complete and implement the Unicorn Leader Action Steps. My hope is that you will take intentional actions focused on self-improvement, helping others, and continued learning that will allow you to manifest the universe and live the magical life you deserve to live.

The Unicorn Leadership journey continues for me. There is still so much to learn, so many more books to read, and so many more people to help. And, of course, more self-work and improvement needs to be done. I would love to learn from you! Please reach out to me via email at anne@annewitherspoon.com or on Instagram @ unicornleadership101 and share your feedback, experiences, and leadership insight. I wish you much success in your future and much magic in your own journey.

Map Your (Unicorn Leader) Journey

Cat: Where are you going?
Alice: Which way should I go?
Cat: That depends on where you are going.
Alice: I don't know.
Cat: Then it doesn't matter which way you go.
—LEWIS CARROLL, *ALICE IN WONDERLAND*

To be a Unicorn Leader requires a clear understanding of where you are going and being able to articulate how you are going to get there.

Based on my values of

And my strengths of

My BHAG is

The person I admire who is amazing in this area and is the poster child is

The skills or credentials I currently possess are

The skills or credentials I must acquire are

The contacts that could help me with advice, coaching, or mentorship are

Some networking ideas I have that could help me connect with others in this area are

A few self-care items (better health, eating habits, more sleep, etc.) I need to address to get where I'm going are

My timeline is

The determined actions I will take are

30 days

90 days

180 days

One year+

A quote to inspire me in this quest is

The feeling(s) I will experience when my BHAG is accomplished is/are

Some obstacles I will probably encounter are

My plan to overcome the obstacles, the haters, and everything in between is

Unicorn Leader Action Steps

You are what you repeatedly do. Excellence is not a singular act but a habit.
—ARISTOTLE

Begin to magically unlock the power of the universe with intentional actions! #manifesttheuniverse

1. Determine your personal values.
2. Learn your organizational and team member values and determine how/whether values align.
3. Take personality assessments with your team members; discuss assessment results, display results, and adjust your style for better interaction.
4. Determine your strengths utilizing StrengthsFinder and/or StandOut assessments.
5. Learn your team members' strengths; discuss strengths, display strengths, and find opportunities for those strengths to be used.
6. Sign up for the Freethinking Leader Coalition at www.freethinkingleader.org.
7. Complete the Performance Tracker and the Genius Habit Questionnaire at www.lauragarnett.com.
8. Read *The Ideal Team Player*; review resources at www.tablegroup.com.

9. Pay attention to your culture; take the Founder's Mentality Diagnostic Survey at media.bain.com/founders-mentality/.
10. Read *First, Break All the Rules*. Ask your team the twelve questions; determine the areas of success and also those that need attention.
11. Get to know your team and build trust; learn about your team and what makes them unique individuals.
12. Read *The Five Dysfunctions of a Team*; complete the assessment and review resources at www.tablegroup.com.
13. Gather your team members' birthdays and work anniversaries and recognize these occasions in some way.
14. Document a list of the "favorite things" of team members; incorporate these items into recognition and celebration events.
15. Celebrate important things with your team: birthdays, work anniversaries, results, successes. Incorporate fun into your work.
16. Conduct Stay Interviews with your team members.
17. Meet with your team members regularly; give them your attention and ask how you can help them.
18. Take steps to educate, train, and develop your team on various topics (skills, leadership, industry, etc.).
19. Schedule some fun at work! This could be almost anything, including lunch, bowling, running, community service, coffee, an escape room, or an afternoon at the park. Celebrate a "fun" national holiday such as National Unicorn Day (April 9).
20. Watch content at www.fishphilosophy.com/ and incorporate Play! into your workday.
21. Watch content at www.radicalcandor.com.

22. Watch the interview of Alan Mulally on *Jay Leno's Garage* for leadership inspiration: www.youtube.com/watch?v=u4aatqMxFnE.
23. Read *The Truth about Employee Engagement*. Take steps to avoid job misery: get to know your employees, help them see their work has purpose, and show their progress toward goals.
24. Read Tim Urban's article "Your Life in Weeks." Order a Life Calendar and be mindful of each week in your life: waitbutwhy.com/2014/05/life-weeks.html.
25. Take steps to build a strong physical foundation: exercise, healthy eating, adequate sleep.
26. Improve your emotional and mental capacity: listen to music, meditate, journal, breathe, do more of what you love.
27. Take an EQ Assessment at www.mindtools.com or at www.talentsmarteq.com/test/.
28. Take the Insight Quiz at www.tashaeurich.com to determine your current level of self-awareness; consider completing the Future-Ready Leader course or the activities in the appendix of the book *Insight: The Surprising Truth About How Others See Us, How We See Ourselves, and Why the Answers Matter More Than We Think.*
29. Take the 360-Degree Leadership skills assessment at www.360DegreeLeader.com.
30. Reach out to five people who have been instrumental in your career and/or life success; tell them thank you, invite them to coffee, or send them a note to show you appreciate their positive impact on your life.

31. Take the Mindset Assessment at http://blog.mindsetworks.com/

what-s-my-mindset and explore resources and tools to help develop your growth mindset.

32. Read *What Got You Here Won't Get You There: How Successful People Become Even More Successful.* Review Marshall Goldsmith's "The 20 Bad Habits" at www.marshallgoldsmith.com/wp-content/uploads/2017/01/Marshall-Goldsmith-20-Bad-Habits-1.pdf and take steps to break any limitations you have.
33. Create a vision board that illustrates your hopes, dreams, and aspirations.
34. Consider getting guidance from a mentor, executive coach, or life coach to help you become the best leader and person you can be.
35. Learn more about self-compassion at www.selfcompassion.org or www.centerformsc.org.
36. Watch the Netflix series *Headspace: Guide to Meditation.*
37. Take time to "be kind to yourself" and exercise, meditate, write in a journal, or express gratitude.
38. Take the Badass Workshop at www.badassworkshop.com, curated by Bozoma Saint John.
39. Watch Simon Sinek's TED Talk on why good leaders make you feel safe: www.ted.com/talks/simon_sinek_why_good_leaders_make_you_feel_safe.
40. Use WOOP (Wish, Outcome, Obstacle, Plan) to find and fulfill your wishes: woopmylife.org/en/home.

References, Recommended Reading, and Resources

Chapter One: Values

Chapman, Gary and Campbell, Ross. *The 5 Love Languages of Children: The Secret to Loving Children Effectively*. Chicago: Northfield Publishing, 2016.

Covey, Sean. *The 7 Habits of Happy Kids*. New York: Simon & Schuster Books for Young Readers, 2008.

Hsieh, Tony. *Delivering Happiness*. New York: Grand Central Publishing, 2010.

Lencioni, Patrick. *The 3 Big Questions for a Frantic Family: A Leadership Fable . . . About Restoring Sanity to the Most Important Organization in Your Life*. San Francisco: Jossey-Bass, 2008.

Rhoades, Ann. *Built on Values: Creating an Enviable Culture That Outperforms the Competition*. San Francisco: Jossey-Bass. 2010.

Stassen, Jan. "Why Values Matter." Video. www.youtube.com/watch?v=_a1Fc6nwpks.

Chapter Two: Know Yourself

Buckingham, Marcus. *StandOut 2.0*. Boston: Harvard Business Review Press, 2015.

Buckingham, Marcus, and Ashley Goodall. *Nine Lies about Work: A Freethinking Leader's Guide to the Real World*. Boston: Harvard Business Review Press, 2019.

Clifton, Don. *StrengthsFinder 2.0*. New York: Gallup Press, 2007.

Dawdy, Gwynne N. *The Social Compass: Time Tested Methods to Communicate Better, Understand Others, Resolve Conflict & Keep Your Project and Team at the Top*. Shelbyville, KY: Wasteland Press, 2006.

Garnett, Laura. *The Genius Habit: How One Habit Can Radically Change Your Work and Your Life*. Naperville, IL: Sourcebooks, 2019. www.lauragarnett.com

Harvard Business Review. "Freethinking Leader Coalition." Accessed October 30, 2021. freethinkingleader.org.

www.leadrighttoday.com

www.marcusbuckingham.com

www.myersbriggs.org

Chapter Three: Culture

Gordon, Jon. *The Energy Bus: 10 Rules to Fuel Your Life, Work, and Team with Positive Energy*. Hoboken, NJ: Wiley, 2007.

Lencioni, Patrick. *The Ideal Team Player: How to Recognize and Cultivate the Three Essential Virtues*. Hoboken, NJ: Jossey-Bass, 2016.

media.bain.com/founders-mentality/

Sinek, Simon. "How Great Leaders Inspire Action." Filmed September 2009 at TEDxPuget Sound, Newcastle, WA. Video. www.ted.com/talks/simon_sinek_how_great_leaders_inspire_action.

Sinek, Simon. *Leaders Eat Last: Why Some Teams Pull Together and Others Don't*. New York: Penguin Random House, 2014, 2017.

www.tablegroup.com

www.TheEnergyBus.com

Zappos.com. *Zappos 2014 Culture Book, The Next Chapter.* Las Vegas: Zappos.com, 2014.

Zook, Chris and James Allen. *The Founder's Mentality: How to Overcome the Predictable Crises of Growth.* Boston: Harvard Business Review Press, 2016.

Chapter Four: Teamwork

Berger, Warren. *The Book of Beautiful Questions: The Powerful Questions That Will Help You Decide, Create, Connect, and Lead.* New York: Bloomsbury Publishing. 2018.

Buckingham, Marcus. *First, Break All the Rules: What the World's Greatest Managers Do Differently.* New York: Gallup Press, 2016.

Buckingham, Marcus and Ashley Goodall. *Nine Lies About Work: A Freethinking Leader's Guide to the Real World.* Boston: Harvard Business Review Press, 2019.

Clifton, Jim and Jim Harter. *It's the Manager: Moving from Boss to Coach.* New York: Gallup Press, 2019.

Friedman, Ron. *The Best Place to Work: The Art and Science of Creating an Extraordinary Workplace.* New York: TarcherPerigee, 2014.

Gostick, Adrian and Chester Elton. *The Best Team Wins: The New Science of High Performance.* New York: Simon & Schuster, 2018.

Lencioni, Patrick. *The Five Dysfunctions of a Team: A Leadership Fable.* San Francisco: Jossey-Bass, 2002.

Lipp, Doug. *Disney U: How Disney University Develops the World's Most Engaged, Loyal, and Customer-Centric Employees*. New York: McGraw Hill, 2013.

Sinek, Simon. "Why Good Leaders Make You Feel Safe." Filmed March 2014 at TED2014. www.ted.com/talks/simon_sinek_why_good_leaders_make_you_feel_safe.

www.tablegroup.com

Chapter Five: Have Fun

AdultingFTW.com

Hsieh, Tony. *Delivering Happiness: A Path to Profits, Passion, and Purpose*. New York: Grand Central Publishing, 2010.

Lundin, Stephen C., Harry Paul, and John Christensen. *FISH!: A Proven Way to Boost Morale and Improve Results*. New York: Hachette Go, 2000. www.fishphilosophy.com/fish-philosophy-story/.

Chapter Six: Provide Feedback

Alan Mulally on *Jay Leno's Garage* www.youtube.com/watch?v=u4aatqMxFnE.

Hoffman, Bryce G. *American Icon: Alan Mulally and the Fight to Save Ford Motor Company*. New York: Crown Business, 2012.

www.radicalcandor.com

Scott, Kim. *Radical Candor: Be a Kick-Ass Boss without Losing Your Humanity*. New York: St. Martin's Press, 2019.

www.tablegroup.com

Chapter Seven: Employee Engagement

AJR. "BANG!" Video. www.youtube.com/watch?v=4THFRpw68oQ.

Clifton, Jim and Jim Harte. *It's the Manager: Moving from Boss to Coach.* New York: Gallup Press, 2019.

Lencioni, Patrick. *The Truth about Employee Engagement: A Fable about Addressing the Three Root Causes of Job Misery.* San Francisco: Jossey-Bass, 2015.

Urban, Tim. "Your Life In Weeks," *Wait But Why* (blog), 2014, www.waitbutwhy.com/2014/05/life-weeks.html.

Chapter Eight: Mental Toughness

Buckingham, Marcus and Ashley Goodall. *Nine Lies About Work: A Freethinking Leader's Guide to the Real World.* Boston: Harvard Business Review Press, 2019.

Goldsmith, Marshall. *Triggers: Creating Behavior That Lasts—Becoming the Person You Want to Be.* New York: Crown Publishing Group, 2015.

Harvard Business Review. *HBR's 10 Must Reads on Mental Toughness.* Boston: Harvard Business Review Press, 2018.

Irvine, William B. *The Stoic Challenge: A Philosopher's Guide to Becoming Tougher, Calmer, and More Resilient.* New York: W. W. Norton & Company, 2019.

Itzler, Jesse. *Living with a SEAL: 31 Days Training with the Toughest Man on the Planet.* New York: Hachette Book Group, 2015.

Loehr, Jim and Tony Schwartz. "The Making of a Corporate Athlete," *Harvard Business Review,* January 2001, hbr.org/2001/01/the-making-of-a-corporate-athlete.

Schlueter, Apryl Zarate. *Finding Success in Balance: My Journey to the Cheerful Mind*. Northbrook, IL: The Cheerful Mind, Inc., 2017.

www.calm.com

Chapter Nine: Perspective

Bradberry, Travis and Jean Greaves. *Emotional Intelligence 2.0*. San Diego: TalentSmart, 2009.

Ehrenreich, Barbara. *Nickel and Dimed: On (Not) Getting By in America*. New York: Picador USA, 2011.

Emotional Intelligence 2.0 book and assessment available at www.talentsmarteq.com/test/

Eurich, Tasha. *Insight: The Surprising Truth About How Others See Us, How We See Ourselves, and Why the Answers Matter More Than We Think*. New York: Crown Publishing Group, 2017.

Eurich, Tasha. The Insight Course, theinsightcourse.com/.

Goleman, Daniel. *Social Intelligence: The New Science of Human Relationships*. New York: Bantam, 2006.

Harvard Business Review. *HBR's 10 Must Reads on Emotional Intelligence*. Boston: Harvard Business Review Press, 2015.

Kahneman, Daniel and Angus Deaton. "High Income Improves Evaluation of Life But Not Emotional Well-Being," 2010, www.pnas.org/doi/10.1073/pnas.1011492107.

McCollough, Jack. *The Psychopathic CEO: An Executive Survival Guide*. 2021.

www.mindtools.com

Ronson, Jon. *The Psychopath Test: A Journey through the Madness Industry*. Riverhead Books, 2011.

Sarkis, Stephanie. "Senior Leaders are More Likely to be Psychopaths," *Forbes*, October 27, 2019, www.forbes.com/sites/stephaniesarkis/2019/10/27/senior-executives-are-more-likely-to-be-psychopaths/?sh=61ed718947c4.

www.TashaEurich.com

Chapter Ten: Relationships

Carnegie, Dale. *How to Win Friends & Influence People*. New York: Simon & Schuster, 1936.

Ferrazzi, Keith and Tahl Raz. *Never Eat Alone: And Other Secrets to Success, One Relationship at a Time*. New York: Crown Publishing Group, 2001.

Maxwell, John C. *The 360 Degree Leader: Developing Your Influence from Anywhere in the Organization*. Nashville: Thomas Nelson Inc, 2005. www.360DegreeLeader.com.

Chapter Eleven: Evolve

Dweck, Carol S. *Mindset. The New Psychology of Success*. New York: Random House, 2006.

Goldsmith, Marshall. *What Got You Here Won't Get You There: How Successful People Become Even More Successful*. New York: Hachette Books, 2007.

Johnson, Spencer. *Who Moved My Cheese?* New York: G. P. Putnam's Sons, 1998.

Kotter, John P. *Leading Change*. Boston: Harvard Business Review Press, 2012.

Kotter, John P. and Holger Rathgeber. *Our Iceberg Is Melting*. New York: St. Martin's Press, 2005.

Kubler-Ross Change Curve, 1969, www.ekrfoundation.org.

Maxwell, John C. *The 360 Degree Leader: Developing Your Influence from Anywhere in the Organization*. Nashville: Thomas Nelson Inc, 2005.

www.mindsetworks.com

Rhimes, Shonda. *Year of Yes: How to Dance It Out, Stand in the Sun and Be Your Own Person*. New York: Simon & Schuster, 2015.

Schmidt, Eric, Jonathan Rosenberg, and Alan Eagle. *Trillion Dollar Coach: The Leadership Playbook of Silicon Valley's Bill Campbell*. New York: Harper Business, 2019.

Wedell, Gavin. "Change Management Explained in 1 Minute." www.youtube.com/watch?v=gmoDpj1jtyA

Chapter Twelve: Self-Compassion

Achor, Shawn. *The Happiness Advantage: How a Positive Brain Fuels Success in Work and Life*. New York: Crown Business, 2010.

Brown, Brene. *The Gifts of Imperfection: Let Go of Who You Think You're Supposed to Be and Embrace Who You Are*. Center City, MN: Hazelden Publishing, 2010.

Brown, Brene. *I Thought It Was Just Me (But It Isn't): Making the Journey from "What Will People Think?" to "I Am Enough."* New York: Avery, 2007.

centerformsc.org/

Collins, Jim. *Good to Great: Why Some Companies Make the Leap . . . and Others Don't*. New York: Harper Business, 2001.

www.coursera.com

www.headspace.com

www.selfcompassion.org

Chapter Thirteen: Authentic Leadership

Doyle, Glennon. *Untamed*. The Dial Press, 2020.

Durrwachter, Dianna. "Authentic Leadership." Filmed October 2020 at TEDxWilliamsport. Video. www.ted.com/talks/dianna_durrwachter_authentic_leadership.

Frei, Frances X. and Anne Morriss. *Unleashed: The Unapologetic Leader's Guide to Empowering Everyone Around You*. Boston: Harvard Business Review Press, 2020.

Ibarra, Herminia. "What Does It Really Mean for Leaders to Be Authentic?" Filmed May 2018 at TEDxLondonBusinessSchool. www.ted.com/talks/herminia_ibarra_what_does_it_really_mean_for_leaders_to_be_authentic.

Jones, Luvvie Ajayi. *Professional Troublemaker: The Fear-Fighter Manual*. New York: Penguin Life, 2021.

Karajagi, Niket. "Authentic Leadership." Filmed August 2018 at TEDxKLSGIT. www.ted.com/talks/niket_karajagi_authentic_leadership.

Saint John, Bozoma. The Badass Workshop, www.thebadassworkshop.com.

Sinek, Simon. "Why Good Leaders Make You Feel Safe." Filmed May 19, 2014, at TED.

www.ted.com/talks/simon_sinek_why_good_leaders_make_you_feel_safe.

Chapter Fourteen: Courage

Bechtle, Dr. Mike. *People Can't Drive You Crazy If You Don't Give Them the Keys*. Grand Rapids, MI: Revell, 2012.

Brown, Brene. *Daring Greatly: How the Courage to Be Vulnerable Transforms the Way We Live, Love, Parent, and Lead*. New York: Avery, 2012.

Collings, James C. and Jerry I. Porras. *Built to Last: Successful Habits of Visionary Companies*. New York: Harper Business, 1994.

Doyle, Glennon. *Untamed*. The Dial Press, 2020.

Gleeson, Brent. *Embrace the Suck: The Navy SEAL Way to an Extraordinary Life*. New York: Hachette Book Group, 2020.

Irvine, William B. *The Stoic Challenge: A Philosopher's Guide to Becoming Tougher, Calmer, and More Resilient*. New York: W. W. Norton & Company, 2019.

Jones, Luvvie Ajayi. Professional Troublemaker. *The Fear-Fighter Manual*. New York: Penguin Life, 2021.

www.njlifehacks.com/woop-goal-setting-method/

Pressfield, Steven. *The War of Art: Break Through the Blocks and Win Your Inner Creative Battles*. New York: Black Irish Entertainment LLC, 2002.

www.woopmylife.org/en/home

Acknowledgments

Dreams can come true but not without a lot of help, faith, support, and love from multiple people along the way. Many thanks to my husband, Jonathan, for providing encouragement throughout the entire process. He's the only one who has witnessed my entire leadership journey and has been there to help me in good times and not-so-good times. Thanks to my children, John and Ellen, for humoring me by listening to my many "leadership nuggets" and mocking me with only love and kindness.

I'm inspired by the never-ending patience and support of my besties, fabulous friends, and BFFs. I'm thankful for my mentors and champions who helped me do better and be better. I'm grateful for my colleagues who embraced my ideas and allowed me to add value and be valued. I could not have done this without the direction and expertise of Joann Dobbie, Kim Bookless, and Bethany Brown. A huge thank-you to Apryl Schlueter for all her positive energy and inspiration. Special thanks to Michael Clinton for his generosity and guidance.

Thanks to all my family and friends who believed in me and cheered me on during the ups and downs along the way—I am forever grateful. Thank you to all the authors and leaders I have referenced throughout. Your research, inspiration, achievements, and direct—or indirect—guidance have been invaluable.

Author Bio

Anne Witherspoon is a C-level leader who loves to learn. *Unicorn Leadership* is her first book. It was a bucket list item to get all the nuggets of experience out of her head and on to paper. She has spent the past twenty-five-plus years working in corporate America and learning from the best and the worst. She has multiple professional certifications and has read hundreds of books on her quest to become the very best leader that she can be. Her journey is far from over!

She believes it is possible to #ManifestTheUniverse with intentional actions. Her favorite song of all time is "Dream On" by Steven Tyler, and she wants to remind everyone to *"dream until your dream comes true."*

Connect with her and send her your personal nuggets of experiences, best practices, and feedback at @unicornleadership101 on Instagram, visit her website at www.annewitherspoon.com, or email her at anne@annewitherspoon.com.

Printed in Great Britain
by Amazon

57737525R00089